IN THE FAMILY OF MOTORCYCLISTS, TOURING RIDERS ARE UNIQUE. THEY

are very discerning, vocal with their opinions, and among the most knowledgeable about their own

special kind of riding. Without them, the Gold Wing never would have evolved into what it is

today, and for that reason it stands alone, unique among motorcycles.   The Gold Wing

is a true motorcycle of the people, shaped, focused and tailored for 20 years by the special

demands of touring riders, and designed and built by people

who share their vision. No other motor-

cycle has so depended on people for

its very existence. And no other motor-

cycle has so completely embodied the unique,

American spirit of long-distance riding.   That spirit is alive in Marysville and

Anna, Ohio, where Gold Wings are made by Americans who take tremendous pride in

creating this special machine.   This book celebrates the first 20 years of the Gold

Wing, and of that special relationship between the people who build it and the people who ride it.

   Thank you for helping us create this legendary motorcycle.

Best regards,

Koichi Amemiya
President, American Honda Motor Co., Inc.

FOREWORD

IN THE FAMILY OF MOTORCYCLISTS, TOURING RIDERS ARE UNIQUE. THEY are very discerning, vocal with their opinions, and among the most knowledgeable about their own special kind of riding. Without them, the Gold Wing never would have evolved into what it is today, and for that reason it stands alone, unique among motorcycles.   The Gold Wing is a true motorcycle of the people, shaped, focused and tailored for 20 years by the special demands of touring riders, and designed and built by people who share their vision. No other motorcycle has so depended on people for its very existence. And no other motorcycle has so completely embodied the unique American spirit of long-distance riding.   That spirit is alive in Marysville and Anna, Ohio, where Gold Wings are made by Americans who take tremendous pride in creating this special machine.   This book celebrates the first 20 years of the Gold Wing, and of that special relationship between the people who build it and the people who ride it.

Thank you for helping us create this legendary motorcycle.

Best regards,

Koichi Amemiya
President, American Honda Motor Co., Inc.

Published for American Honda Motor Co., Inc. by
VREEKE & ASSOCIATES

•

KEN VREEKE • Editor-in-Chief
CHARLES EVERITT • Managing Editor
HEATHER HANE-KARR • Art Director

•

AMERICAN HONDA MOTOR CO., INC.
Publisher

•

CONTRIBUTORS
Rich Cox • Kevin Wing • Jerry Garns • Bill Delaney • Greg Alter
Robin Riggs • Jim Miller • Jerry Smith • Jeff Karr • *Motorcyclist* magazine
Rider magazine • *Cycle World* magazine • *Cycle* magazine
Gold Wing Road Riders Association

•

© 1994, American Honda Motor Co., Inc.,
1919 Torrance Blvd., Torrance, CA 90501, U.S.A.

Printed and bound in the U.S.A.

Library of Congress Catalog Card Number: 94-72691: Vreeke, Ken

Gold Wing. The First 20 Years. Official publication by American Honda Motor Co., Inc.: Vreeke, Ken

ISBN 0-9642491-0-3

$\mathcal{I}$ NTRODUCTION

SHORTLY AFTER ENTERING THE conference room in Honda's R&D center in Asaka-dai, Japan—birthplace of the Gold Wing—our Japanese liaison leaned toward me and whispered, "I think there are only about four bikes in all of Honda's history that were not designed by someone in this room."

Around the table sat 22 men. Introductions connected faces to machines: the exotic, oval-piston NR750; the CX650 Turbo; the CB77 Super Hawk; the CB750 four-cylinder; the fabled CBX six. There were many more legendary motorcycles represented by the men in this room, but they all had one particular machine in common: the Gold Wing.

Today, Honda is a multinational corporation with thousands of products to its credit. But back in 1973 when the Gold Wing was conceived, a young Honda Motor Company was just beginning to explore the depths of its engineering talent. Honda counted its projects by number, and the Gold Wing was known internally as Project 371. It's difficult to imagine such a ground-breaking motorcycle could have sprung from a company just beginning to mature. Certainly, those involved in creating the original Gold

Wing more than 20 years ago could hardly have envisioned what the bike would become.

Twenty years after its introduction, the Gold Wing has secured a place in history as a singular, enduring achievement, a machine that forged a new path in motorcycle design, and one that played a key role in Honda's success in America, helping to transform the small American distributor with eight employees and a line of six machines into an industry giant.

Much has been written about the Gold Wing in the 20 years since it first appeared at the Cologne show in October 1974. This 20th anniversary commemorative Gold Wing book could not be a rehash of existing information, though. From the outset, we wanted to tell the Gold Wing story from the perspective of those who created it, and in the process perhaps learn more about the way Honda builds motorcycles.

To accomplish this, access to Honda R&D was essential. The real story of the Gold Wing was in the heads of the men who created it. But like most major industrial concerns, Honda is not in the habit of throwing open its R&D centers to prying journalists.

On our first of several trips to Japan to research the book, we didn't know quite what to expect. Yet at Asaka-dai, we were greeted with an openness normally reserved for insiders. Engineers, designers, test riders and project leaders whose imagination and skill shaped the Gold Wing from the very beginning became the source for much of the material in the book. There was the rare, grainy black-and-white photograph taken in a dimly lit engineering room. Or a wild styling sketch that never made it off the drawing board. The mock-up that never made production. Material that had never breached the airtight security of Honda R&D.

As we began to interview these men, something not often associated with industrialized Japan began to emerge: passion. Rather than a stiff recitation of facts, personal stories of the Gold Wing unfolded.

There was the story, recalled in vivid detail by the young engineer in charge of developing the shaft drive system—Honda's first—for the Gold Wing. He would spend months creating a new design only to watch test riders destroy his best work over and over again. Three years and a trail of countless broken gears and cases later, Honda had its first motorcycle shaft drive. Why not simply borrow existing technology? Mr. Honda had always instilled a belief that you cannot advance current design without first mastering the fundamentals. For one young Gold Wing engineer, that meant living in a gearcase for two torturous years.

For the GL1500, final design sketches showed smooth, fully enclosed bodywork with no visible fasteners. No magical computer program exists to figure out how to fasten the bodywork. Instead, we heard the story of the engineer in charge of solving the problem, who locked himself in a rural cottage away from the distractions of work and friends for three months before emerging with every bracket, every fitment, every fastener sketched out.

This hands-on, human approach to development is evident throughout the Gold Wing story, and it permeates the highest levels of management. Every Gold Wing project leader, for example, had vast riding—if not racing—experience. When a decision had to be made about a design direction at a crucial prototype stage, it was not uncommon for the project leader to saddle up and experience firsthand what testers were talking about before making a decision. Honda comes by this hands-on style naturally, a result of Mr. Honda's quickness to get his hands around a new part, his mind around a new problem.

Many of the men who played a role in the Gold Wing went on to other successes. One young development engineer on the original Gold Wing team went on to become vice president of Honda Racing Corporation. Despite a career that boasts many World Championships, he recalled the Gold Wing project with great animation, and still regards his contribution to the Gold Wing as one of his greatest accomplishments.

One by one, the stories came tumbling out with an enthusiasm all too often hidden behind corporate formalities: late nights working through a gearcase problem, developing a new method of testing, chipping away at a clay mock-up to get just the right curve of a

fuel tank. These were not corporate men merely doing a job. There was real enthusiasm here, the kind you see whenever people gather to talk about motorcycles.

Over the course of several months and several trips to Japan and Ohio—where more than 400,000 Gold Wings have been produced since 1975—we interviewed hundreds of people who played a role in the Gold Wing story. All recall it with the kind of pride that comes from creating something with your own hands.

The Gold Wing is and always will be held in special regard at Honda. In a fast-changing marketplace, the Gold Wing has an enduring, endearing identity, the personal stamp of those who created it, and those who continue to carry the torch.   —Ken Vreeke

"BEFORE TECHNOLOGY, THERE MUST BE

A WAY OF THINKING." —*Soichiro Honda*

THE ORIGINAL: PART ONE

FROM THE M1 TO THE PRODUCTION LINE.

FOR A JAPANESE COMPANY TO BUILD A long-distance touring motorcycle—even now, let alone 20 years ago—requires an improbably wild stretch of the imagination, as though an Inuit from above the Arctic Circle were to bring out a line of bathing suits. Densely crowded Japan is the antithesis of wide-open space, a place in which Grand Touring can hardly even be imagined, now or then.

Nevertheless, Honda did make that leap of imagination, and did produce the most successful touring motorcycle of all time—a machine that literally defined the present touring culture. In 20 years of production, Honda's Gold Wing series has been its most durable and profitable motorcycle line. The GL's long production run led to the current concept of continuous refinement, which is now central to success in every vehicle market. During those many years of production, Gold Wings have been primary proof of Honda quality and durability.

In the beginning, though, there existed only a resolve to build something fine and admirable: It was called the King of Kings, code name M1. This is how Honda's engineers remember it and this is how they tell it. The prototype they called M1 was the result of ambition, not of focus groups or marketing studies. The M1 was conceived as the "King of the Motorcycles."

ALTHOUGH IT LED TO THE GOLD WING, THE M1 was never a Gold Wing prototype. Instead, the M1, with its liquid-cooled 1470cc flat-six engine, was meant to probe the limits of possibility in motorcycle design— to be the King of Kings motorcycle.

THE M1'S LIQUID-COOLED ENGINE PIONEERED several features that would reappear in the GL1500 years later, such as the flat-six architecture and the coolant-heated intake manifold to promote consistent fuel/air mixture under diverse conditions.

THE M1 AS IT LIVES TODAY, PHOTOGRAPHED outside Honda's R&D facility in Japan. It now wears a complete front end from a GL1100, in place of the CB750 components it had originally. This engine was also used in a GL1200 chassis to test the concept of the GL1500, making it one of the longest-lived testing mules in Honda history.

At that time—more than 20 years ago now—new projects at Honda were engineering-driven, not the result of market analysis. Projects were proposed because they were possible. It had been this kind of thinking that led to creation of the CB750, a motorcycle so complex for its time that expert opinion in the established industry denied it could ever be sold at a profit. Such thinking parallels successful developments in the aircraft industry. The most successful civil transport aircraft have been the engineering-driven designs; not designs created to please existing markets.

Engineering-driven development's great strength is that it explores the barely possible, rather than restricting itself to the presently desirable. The market can make a choice among existing alternatives, but has no knowledge of the future. In dealing with emerging technologies, engineers can actively create a future consumers can barely imagine.

This is a key element of the multifaceted Honda Way: to ignore existing boundaries and push toward the unexplored, then build it and see what can be applied to production. One of Mr. Honda's philosophies that defined the Honda Way was first to always do or make something. Next, think and consider and revise. It's a philosophy that guides the company today.

You can see evidence of that thinking in the biannual All-Honda Idea Contest, where employees are encouraged to let their imaginations run wild, and build whatever they can dream up; some ideas even eventually see production.

It was engineering-driven development that led to the development of the company's ultra-advanced, multi-cylinder GP race bikes in the 1960s, which mapped the future by extending the range of the possible. To create these machines, Honda's engineers had to master the art of making extremely complex castings,

Honda was the number one motorcycle manufacturer in the world, and it wanted to make a flagship.

But what physical form should such a divine motorcycle take? Not even Honda knew at that time. In those days, as one engineer put it, "Honda did not have any concept of what is King of Motorcycling. We didn't know. That's why we made this prototype motorcycle [M1]." In other words, the M1 was to be Honda's techno-sounding board; outrageous experimentation, simply for its own sake.

The design team was assembled in December of 1972. At its head was a young but brilliant engineer named Shoichiro Irimajiri, who had led the design of Honda's classic five- and six-cylinder GP road racing engines of the 1960s, and had then gone on to assist in Honda's transition to automobile manufacturing. At the time, the M1 was intended to be a Grand Touring model, superior to all others in smoothness, comfort, specifications, and quality.

AS THE M1 SLOWLY begins to take shape, you can see design elements that will trickle down to the Gold Wing: the steel-tube frame, horizontally opposed engine layout, shaft drive, disc front brake and—years later— saddlebags.

and they did so where possible by developing production techniques, rather than using hand methods. In this way, the racing development actually became the investment that would make the CB750 and later complex models possible.

In 1972, Honda maintained a force of about 1000 R&D specialists at its Wako engineering center. In those days, engineers all worked in the same room, not grouped in separate departments. This partitionless arrangement was intentional, the expression of Mr. Honda's insistence upon *zakku-baran*, or openness, frankness, so that almost everyone could participate in the decision-making process. This unregimented mass of engineering talent was, therefore, a marvelous university for engineering of all kinds, an opportunity for a young engineer to be exposed to every kind of project—motorcycle design, racing, automobile development, and more. Combine this with the founder's insistence that talent be judged by accomplishment and not by age or authority, and the potential for innovation is limitless.

It was to explore extremes that the M1 was first built with a flat-six engine. Another consideration was the smoothness of the rotary engine, in 1972 quite a fashionable idea in motorcycling. Was it even possible to equal the rotary with any form of piston engine? A six had the best chance.

It is surprising today to look at the official goals for the M1, which called for a very compact and light machine of extremely high performance. It was to weigh 463 pounds, divided roughly 40/60-percent between engine and chassis. Power was targeted at 61 bhp at a high, 7500 rpm, with maximum torque given not at highway cruising rpm, but much higher up the scale at 5500. Most telling was the quarter-mile performance goal of 12.40 seconds—quicker than the CB750. Obviously, the M1 project was more than pure experimentation: The Kawasaki Z-1 had just been released, which outpowered Honda's own, epoch-making CB750.

Viewed as Grand Tourers, the existing machines of that time had serious problems. BMWs were expensive, the Harleys of that time had a reputation for requiring considerable maintenance, and so on. Conversely, each also had certain strengths, possibly

EARLY DESIGN SKETCHES SHOW JUST HOW many different visions Honda had of the Gold Wing's role, and how diverse they were. There was endless discussion among top management at Honda as to just what this new motorcycle should be: supersport, or Grand Tourer. In pushing toward the latter, with a powerband that emphasized mid-range, Honda was taking a great risk in a marketplace enamored with peak performance.

worthy of inclusion in the new design. Entirely fresh ideas, too, were considered.

All previous common motorcycle engines—vertical-twins, flat-twins, V-twins, inline-fours—suffered from either excessive vibration or excessive harsh-

ness. Flat-twins have excellent balance, but, like other twins, they deliver their power in big, solid thuds that reverberate through the vehicle, often annoyingly so. Consequently, the M1 prototype was based on an automotive-style engine of unprecedented smoothness: a liquid-cooled, 1470cc flat-six. The architecture of this engine could deliver both excellent balance and velvety smooth torque, but the selection wasn't initially unanimous among the team. Some were attracted to the compactness of V-twins. Mr. Honda himself, close to retirement from the company he had built, still favored air cooling for its simplicity, and believed that engines larger than 750cc might be rejected by the public as too big.

Indeed, there was friction between the development teams and Mr. Honda over the M1's engine, and some confusion over the M1's mission. As Minoru Matsuda, later in charge of engine design for the GL1000, remembers, the object of the M1's engine was the best power/weight/space ratio, with a wide power range and flat torque curve, not the best power for the displacement. That was almost unheard of, because at the time virtually every manufacturer—Honda included—utilized performance as the key to sales. As for the M1's basic direction, it became split between

THIS EARLY
rendering of the original GL's four-cylinder engine shows the breadth of Honda's vision. The GL was to be a flagship, and had to look the part.

AN EARLY GOLD WING CLAY MOCK-UP SHOWS CB750 influence in fuel tank shape and gaitered fork.

ANOTHER CLAY-MOCK SHOWS EUROPEAN design influence in the shape of the fuel tank, covered fork sliders and bobbed front fender.

the desire to create a Grand Touring machine, and an ultra-high-performance bike.

It's a common misconception that the M1 was the prototype for the GL, and that Honda simply lost its nerve with regard to the six-cylinder engine and produced a four for the Gold Wing. That is not so. Ultimately the M1 was built as a technology demonstrator, an internal showpiece that said, "We can now do this." And it showed that many of the traditional weaknesses of motorcycles were quite unnecessary, that a great leap forward was possible.

The M1 six was given liquid cooling—a radical idea in a time when this technology was the exclusive province of racing engines, automobiles and trucks. Liquid cooling had always been regarded as too complex for so simple and basic a vehicle as a motorcycle. Nevertheless, Honda's engineers knew the operating temperature of air-cooled engines went up and down with air temperature. This was unacceptable for the King of Kings. It must proceed, unaffected and utterly reliable, through the hottest weather and at the highest speeds and loads. With liquid cooling, it would do just that.

Because of the M1 engine's exceptionally low center of gravity, the prototype felt lighter than its true weight of 484 pounds. This, although a byproduct of the design, was so well-liked by those who tested it that it became a focus of the whole design. This, in turn, made greater weights practical.

How many automobile owners would give up their cars if their rear wheels were driven by turn-of-the-century-style open chains? Yet almost all motorcycles were driven in just this way as Honda engineers pondered what the King of Kings would be. The convenience of modern, O-ring-sealed roller chains did not then exist. Aside from its other problems, a chain made noise, required long-term maintenance, and eventually wore out. The King could not have such feet of clay. A sealed, silent and reliable shaft drive was a necessity. Because they didn't have a shaft drive system, engineers used a shaft from a BMW to speed the prototyping process.

The machine Honda engineers envisioned would deliver smooth, effortless and reliable running, yes, but its pipes would speak with authority. This was not to be a King so educated and so civilized that its manners would overshadow its strength and vigor. Everything in Honda's experience told the same story. Riders would not accept a backward step in perfor-

THIS EARLY MOCK-UP IN ROUGH CLAY FORM is one of dozens of three-dimensional design concepts Honda produced before deciding on the GL's look.

mance. The King of Kings would therefore incorporate higher performance than any previous Honda—powerful acceleration and high top speed—as well as all other virtues outlined by the engineers.

For the future of motorcycle touring, the M1 showed that automotive engine technology, with its constant operating temperature, smoothness and silence could be applied to motorcycle design at acceptable levels of weight and complexity. This achievement paralleled that of Honda's CB750, the machine that showed that four cylinders and an overhead camshaft were not too complex or expensive for production motorcycles. For the future of motorcycling in general, the M1 opened the way to the present universal acceptance of largely maintenance-free, liquid-cooled powerplants in bikes of every kind.

Before it could do that, though, it had to pass muster at the highest level. According to legend, *Oyaji* (the Old Man, Mr. Honda himself) appeared unannounced at the test center late one evening. When he saw what his engineers had created, he said with his characteristic rural directness that it "looked like a bat." This was doubtless because of its two wings of three cylinders each. He hopped on the big machine, started it, and rode out into the darkness. Technicians and engineers peered anxiously after him, imagining a disaster for which they would surely be responsible. In due course he returned safely, parked the machine, remarked that it was "pretty good," and went home.

The M1 expanded Honda's sense of what a motorcycle could be, but to derive a marketable product

THIS MOCK-UP, FEATURING A WOOD AND clay engine, shows definite shades of the venerable CB450 in the fuel tank, sidecovers and headlight design. Note enclosed rear shocks and fork sliders.

from that expansion would be difficult. Honda had no touring experience; it was an alien concept. What, if anything, designed for the M1 had practical application in the marketplace?

Clearly, Grand Touring was a theoretical concept in its infancy, while the image of Kawasaki's Z-1 loomed large. Indeed, Honda's aim was to beat against Kawasaki's Z-1 with the CB750 and what would become the GL1000. No doubt Honda engineers were also well aware of BMW's clearly stated goal of combining sport-riding capability with touring smoothness in its then-new /5 models. All of which led to uncertainty about the GL's true role initially, propelled in part by the uncertainty about the M1's. Both were pushed in two directions, high-performance and Grand Touring, and both emphasized more balanced engine performance rather than peak horsepower and class-leading acceleration.

The character of the engine's powerband was partic-

FURTHER ALONG THE PROTOTYPE PROCESS, this mock-up uses real steel in the engine and bodywork. Note the gold wheels and tank-mounted instruments that would appear on later Gold Wings.

EARLY EXPERIMENTS WITH FAIRINGS AND saddlebags didn't come to fruition until Honda introduced the full-dress Interstate in 1980.

ularly risky at the time, and would eventually help define the Gold Wing as a GT bike in the marketplace. There was a clear decision made to distinguish the GL from other motorcycles, but Honda wasn't entirely confident in that decision. As Matsuda says, "There was always someone saying, 'More power, more power.'"

Honda already knew that increased performance with load-carrying ability was simply impossible at the 750cc displacement level of the CB750—or even at 900cc—and they were certain liquid cooling was essential. On the U.S. side, where the muscle-car phenomenon was peaking, thinking was defined by a market focus on performance, far different from the philosophy embodied in the M1, which eschewed top-end power for more balanced engine performance.

While the M1 had been built on a short, 58-inch wheelbase, with its longish engine set end-to-end with the BMW transmission, this design was impossible for a production machine. The rider could not sit close

enough to the front to reach the controls without stretching absurdly compared with riding other bikes of the day. It was also decided that six cylinders were simply too extraordinary for the time, and the market might reject such a design as overly complex.

Engineers drew the first flat-four GL sketches with the transmission positioned behind the engine. But it, too, resulted in an awkward riding position. With their extensive auto engineering background, the engine designers weren't bound by traditional two-wheel thinking, and quickly revised their design to position the transmission under the engine instead of behind it. This innovation permitted the flat engine to clear the rider's shins, while putting the controls comfortably within reach.

Such innovative thinking also led to the GL's underseat fuel tank, though that bit of innovation came about somewhat haphazardly. While BMW's flat engine has its intake system at the rear of the cylinders, both the M1 flat-six and the proposed flat-four

GL engines had to position their carburetors, airbox, and filter system atop the engine. Such a layout competed for space with the fuel tank. According to a styling designer's memory, the GL's fuel tank simply looked grotesquely large at the required capacity. Where to put it? It is part of the GL legend that no less a person than Kiyoshi Kawashima, who would be elevated to the company presidency in 1973, suggested relocating the tank underneath the seat. Can you imagine the high executives of other companies even discussing detailed engineering matters? At Honda, the Old Man and his lieutenants personally toured all departments regularly, discussing development projects with engineers and technicians on a daily basis.

Having positioned the tank under the seat largely for aesthetic reasons, engineers realized a significantly lower center of gravity from the tank's new position. This made the machine feel remarkably lighter than it was. Tadashi Kume, then president of R&D and later president of Honda Motor Co., LTD., sensed the value of this quality and suggested lowering the engine farther, 0.8-inch, to get even more of an already good thing.

The discovery was ironic because it was almost entirely coincidental. Nevertheless, the Gold Wing broke new ground in the field of mass centralization, and pointed a new engineering direction for Honda that continues to be the focus of current motorcycle design.

More daunting were some of the problems Honda discovered simply through a lack of experience. Inexperience with liquid cooling sent Honda testing in the Australian desert summer, where engineers and testers found that if air from the radiator could enter the engine intake, its heat would change carburetor mixture and make the engine run roughly. Yoichi Oguma, then project leader of the testing group and now in command of Honda's racing program, makes a

THE GOLD WING'S FAUX FUEL TANK
featured hinged flanks to provide easy access to
electronics and vital fluids, and a central storage
area for gloves and small items.

masterful understatement when he simply says, "Carburetion was always different." Raising the engine air intake above the hot stream of radiator air helped solve this problem, but it still took about two years to finalize the radiator and coolant plumbing layout.

Likewise, inexperience made development of Honda's own shaft drive system an odyssey for Honda and for engineer Hirotake Takahashi. Oguma recalls that the final drive "broke every day" during development. The engineers devised an *ad-hoc* gear torture which they called "hop test," to simulate the worst of what might happen to gears in

level of silence, reliability, and abuse tolerance. Although Honda could have easily copied existing designs, the GL's shaft drive development was another example of the Honda Way—only by mastering the basics can you build upon future designs.

Just as interesting as what went into the Gold Wing are the items that never made it into production. Engineers considered fuel injection, but discarded it because of the potential problems customers might have with fixing it in the field back in the mid-'70s. Engineers also designed an automatic transmission with an automotive torque convertor, but scrapped the idea due to the high weight and large size; Honda later equipped a version of the CB750 with a two-speed transmission with torque convertor. They also tried a combination hydraulic and electric-motor-powered automatic center-stand—too heavy—and tested an antilock brake system in 1974, but the system was too primitive with then-existing technology.

THE INNOVATIVE GOLD WING ENGINE featured belt-driven cams, which led many testers to speculate on the automobile-division influence on design. In the early days at Honda, automobile and motorcycle R&D departments were under one roof.

DUAL-DISC BRAKES UP FRONT PROVIDED ample stopping power for the Gold Wing, and contributed to its sporty Grand Touring persona.

It was fortunate the GL1000's design reflected many viewpoints, without a completely fixed idea of what it was to be. The resulting machine had a plasticity of purpose that allowed it to be developed in whatever way its customers required. Once the bike was in production, the customers themselves would define the Gold Wing's design direction.

After a short gestation of two years from concept to production, the GL1000 was introduced at the Cologne show in October of 1974. Of all those who saw the machine, few fully understood what it was or might become. For others, who saw it only as straight-line competition for the CB750 and Z-1, it appeared too heavy, too long and too bulky. Once the machines reached U.S. showrooms in 1975, only some 5000 were sold in the first year, far fewer than had been predicted. As one engineer says, "At first, even we didn't have any clear picture of GL customers."

This is not surprising. The public were as mixed in their attitude to the new GL as Honda had been in its creation. What was this machine? Its engine perfor-

actual use. The test rider would coast at a set speed in neutral, then stomp the transmission into first, whereupon the rear wheel would hop violently enough to destroy Takahashi's work. The design and development of power gearing is a special art, and Takahashi had to become a master, altering endless combinations of material, tooth pitch and form, heat treatment, surface hardening. ... After three long years and thousands of combinations, Honda achieved the required high

THE ABOVE MOCK-UP SHOWS AGGRESSIVE styling that takes its cues from Honda's wildly successful CB750 four-cylinder.

THE MAKINGS OF GREATNESS: THIS MOCK-UP begins life with a tube frame and a wood and clay engine. Great care was taken to create accurately proportioned three-dimensional mock-ups to test upper management response to styling.

THIS EARLY MOCK-UP AGAIN SHOWS HONDA'S exploration with design that falls clearly on the side of performance.

mance was second only to the Z-1, and its power came high in the powerband. Yet its weight and size marked it as a touring machine. What was its true calling?

Motorcycle magazines were as confused as anyone else by the Gold Wing. *Cycle's* editors noted that dumping the clutch at 8000 rpm would elicit "150 feet of smoke" from the rear tire, and a 13.0-second/102.38-mph quarter-mile, but at the same time praised the machine as being a clearly focused product—a touring machine.

Of course, in the early 1970s, more than one machine was produced which had no obvious niche. Suzuki's two-stroke GT750 was too ponderous for sport, but was a bit too rough-hewn for touring. Suzuki's rotary suffered the same lack of character definition. Japanese companies were determined to expand the large-displacement market, but unsure of what the new machines should be. Unknown to us all, an era of specialization was dawning. Each of these

bigger bikes was an evolutionary experiment, sent forth to sink or swim in the marketplace. Among these, Honda's GL would flourish and grow.

Despite the slow beginning, the GL's good qualities were recognized by long-distance riders who had tried the alternatives and had found them wanting. Owners discovered the new Honda would carry all the luggage and accessories they needed for longer trips—and they could ride off into the sunset with the same reliability (if not quite the same comfort) as if in the family sedan. This was something entirely new, and touring riders expanded their expectations accordingly.

Indeed, the Gold Wing catalyzed the growth of motorcycle touring in the U.S. Now a rider could have a reliable, capable machine at a reasonable price, and could plan and execute long tours without having to be a tinkerer, and without having to know every dealer along the route. Honda had uncorked a demand previously unexpressed, and people would eventually buy the Gold Wing in droves.

As riders piled up the miles, they also accumulated

suggestions, complaints, wishes. The machine's performance, almost all agreed, was in the wrong place. Could we please trade in some of this quarter-mile performance for enough mid-range punch to pass traffic or climb hills without having to downshift? Another area of improvement was suspension. In the performance era, suspension compliance was not a priority. BMW's machines, though, had soft, long-travel suspension that was praised for its comfort. Harley-Davidsons rolled on bump-eating, large-section tires, and their great weight was less easily disturbed by small bumps. Honda would

have to find its own answers to these problems soon.

Something new was happening. Manufacturers had previously aimed new products at higher levels of performance, and each rise had been greeted with praise. But touring riders did not take this one-dimensional view of the GL; they largely ignored peak performance, and wanted changes in many other areas. Honda had to accommodate itself to this demanding new kind of customer—and indeed to the idea that the customer was becoming a partner in the design process.

DUAL ANALOG DIALS HIGHLIGHTED THE GL'S dash, which included an assortment of warning lights and a temperature gauge in the tachometer. A fuel gauge was located on the top of the faux fuel tank.

FULLY REALIZED, THE GOLD WING HAD A look that was unique and classy. Even today, the original retains its timeless charm.

THE ORIGINAL: PART TWO

TRACING THE EVOLUTION
OF A TOURING DYNASTY.

THE EMERGENCE OF THE GL1000 GOLD WING created a new style of riding in the United States that simply didn't exist before. Certainly, American riders had been touring on a host of other machines, but their numbers were relatively small, and they rarely attempted to travel the kinds of distances the GL's reliability encouraged.

Soon, events, rallies and riding clubs began forming around the Gold Wing, drawing tens of thousands of faithful GL riders. This popularity created a new means of product development: All of a sudden, Honda had the largest fleet of test riders in a company's history—its customers—who would determine the future not only of the Gold Wing, but of the growing touring market itself.

Because the Gold Wing was capable of accommodating such long-distance riding, it came under close scrutiny by customers who piled on the miles. With many motorcycles designed in the late '70s, noise, vibration, lack of top-gear roll-on power, and even suspension harshness were gladly tolerated by customers if the machine had blazing quarter-mile times and looked the part. But touring was a new market where performance alone was not enough.

Minor annoyances were magnified by long hours in the saddle, and by the GL's overall excellence for long-distance riding. In their attempts to modify the factory's design to their needs, owners added such things as stiffer fork springs, fairings, aftermarket rear shocks and custom seats. We know perfection is possible now, they were saying. Give it to us. Honda obliged.

But the development process took time. Until 1978, few changes characterized the GL1000. As customer voices grew louder and more specific, and the

FIRST AND FOURTH GENERATION GOLD Wings, a 1975 GL1000 and a 1988 GL1500, are touring's bookends, illustrating 13 years of development, and the clear influences of thousands of loyal owners.

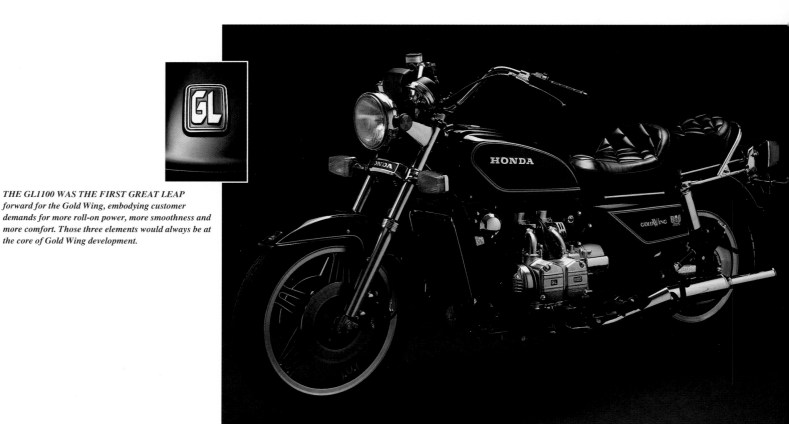

THE GL1100 WAS THE FIRST GREAT LEAP forward for the Gold Wing, embodying customer demands for more roll-on power, more smoothness and more comfort. Those three elements would always be at the core of Gold Wing development.

GL's qualities had been refracted through the prism of the marketplace, Honda implemented bigger changes under engineer Masahiro Senbu for 1978. Not until then did Honda begin with confidence the process of pushing the GL design in the direction its users were exploring on their own. A new way of developing motorcycles was beginning to emerge. As Chief Engineer Tetsuo Mikami says, "Competition did not determine GL development. The reaction of customers made it clear to Honda what direction to take the GL."

For 1978, some of the original machine's high top speed and quarter-mile performance was traded away to gain the stronger roll-on acceleration at cruising speeds customers were clamoring for, a GL development trend that's continued throughout the motorcycle's evolution. The gain was accomplished through smaller carburetors, shorter valve timing and increased spark advance, but gearing remained high, with the engine turning a substantial 3600 rpm at 60 mph. More visible alterations included adopting the front brake system from the latest CB750, and substituting pressed-metal ComStar™ wheels for the original GL's wire-spoke wheels. But of the 1978 model, *Cycle* magazine said, "In its heart and soul the GL1000 still says 1975."

Obviously, there was more work to be done. But 1978 was a pivotal year for the Gold Wing. That was the year all of Japan's big guns fired at once, turning motorcycling into a big-displacement power party. Within the span of about four months, Kawasaki released its Z1-R, Yamaha its XS Eleven, Suzuki its GS1000—and Honda the magnificent six-cylinder CBX™.

The CBX was crucial to the GL's development. Mikami says, "Honda realized the GL really should be developed as a Grand Tourer, not a supersport bike." To compete in the supersport class—and free the GL to pursue the long-distance dictum—Honda began development of the CBX in 1976. That bike's entrance on the scene took the heat off the GL so it could follow its own development path, one that involved refinement rather than complete reconstruction every few years.

Over time, continuous improvement became a new industrial dogma, now widely applied in the auto industry as well. In the past, rapid replacement of one

THE GL1000 LTD OF 1976 WOULD BE THE first of several limited-edition Gold Wings. Honda distinguished this model with special candy-brown paint and gold pin stripes, LTD badges, gold rims and spokes, high-quality show-bike chrome plating, special metallic-silver paint for the engine castings, custom quilt-pattern contoured saddle and a gold-stamped collector's edition owner's manual. Only 2000 were imported into the U.S.

model with another had obscured the possibilities for perfecting existing models and their production process. The success of the Gold Wing kept it in production over years, giving Honda the opportunity to find and address even its smallest flaws. This process showed the value of continuous improvement and product stability, especially important to GL customers who were beginning to resemble a cult following.

As the GL evolved, design contradictions appeared. A major path to reduced vibration is to cut engine cruising rpm by making top gear taller. Yet doing so can also make top-gear roll-on performance more sluggish. Touring riders were already adorning their machines with fairings, luggage and accessories, and often rode two-up far more of the time than Honda expected. This, too, detracted from roll-on passing and hill-climbing performance—and riders complained about it freely.

The 1979 model offered some improvement, but bigger changes were in the making. Engineer Shuji Tanaka, who would be the Gold Wing Large Project Leader for the next five years, is a slight, bespectacled and studious-looking man who would make the GL his own personal expression, and in the process change the direction of the GL forever. Tanaka would come to the U.S. and travel thousands of miles on Gold Wings, and attend touring rallies where he would meet and talk extensively with owners. He practiced *San-Gen-Shugi*, a Honda philosophy of face-to-face research with its customers, a philosophy that leaves nothing lost to other's interpretations. In so doing, Tanaka made himself one of the GL riders' own, and came to see the Gold Wing from the owner's perspective.

For the 1980 model, displacement was pushed to 1085cc and the entire drivetrain was reinforced from crank to output shaft. To accompany the torque-boosting displacement increase, the carburetors were reduced in size yet again, and valve timing and lift were altered, all for better roll-on punch. Fitting an electronic ignition with both centrifugal and vacuum advance also benefited mid-range, and improved fuel economy.

The chassis was simultaneously redesigned as well, establishing future trends of GL development, as customers continued to ask for more comfort, more luxury. A longer wheelbase stretched from the original 60.9 inches to 63.2 to provide more rider and passenger space. Adoption of slippery DU-material (similar to Teflon®) fork bushings smoothed fork action. In this

THE FRONT END OF THIS 1978 GL1000 SHOWS *the twin threads of Honda's development: Pursuit of technology led to the ComStar wheels, while customer requests for more comfort led to continual refinement of the suspension, front and rear.*

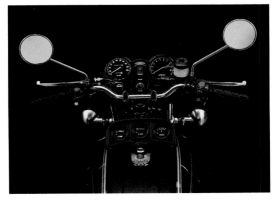

THE GOLD WING RIDER'S OFFICE, CIRCA 1978. *A new tach and speedo with orange-tipped needles greeted the rider, as did a new instrument pod on the tank, with fuel, voltage and temperature gauges.*

era, motorcycle suspension engineers adopted air suspension to handle widely varying loads, and the GL1100 was so equipped, giving the bike its most supple, comfortable ride to date. The verdict? *Cycle* magazine said, "For 1980 Honda has pulled the Gold Wing up by the bootstraps with the reworked engine, suspension system, and accompanying comfort not before associated with Wings. Overwhelmingly, our impressions are favorable—the Gold Wing is, after five years, close to dead-center perfect for its intended use."

While Honda continued to offer a standard GL, 1980 also saw the introduction of the Interstate model, the first Gold Wing with factory-installed fairing and luggage. The machine had evolved into what do-it-yourself users had already made of it: a turn-key, full-dress touring machine of maximum comfort. With the introduction of the 1980 GL1100 Interstate, there were no mods necessary; just load your gear, throw a leg over and go.

Honda's GL1100s showed how much Tanaka had learned, and his ongoing research in the U.S. revealed even more. He discovered, for example, the importance of the passenger. She—usually the wife—not only required long-term comfort and space, but her opinion was often of prime importance in making the original purchase. Just as it had by stretching the wheelbase for 1980 to provide more room, Honda would continue to configure the machine to the pas-

THE 1980s SAW MANUFACTURERS TURN TO *air-assisted suspension to help accommodate varying loads. Honda did so with the GL1100 in 1980, with single-inlet equalizer systems at both ends.*

HONDA RESPONDED TO CUSTOMER DEMANDS with the GL1200 in 1984. The bike once again obliterated existing standards of power, handling and comfort, and reconfirmed the Gold Wing as the king of touring.

senger's needs as well as the rider's. Knowing these unique customer needs was not enough; Tanaka also had to find ways to communicate to higher management the value of such changes. He appointed himself the go-between in a transpacific, cross-cultural exchange.

During the years of Tanaka's stewardship, the GL underwent continuous improvement on every level, beginning with the fundamental changes of 1980. In 1982, the Aspencade was added to the line, and included an on-board air compressor to allow easy alteration of suspension ride height. Alternator output increased to carry the loads imposed by sound systems and other powered accessories. Weight—which began at 584 pounds on the original GL1000—was now up to 702.3 pounds. The Gold Wing had become a big, luxurious motorcycle.

A NEW FAIRING FOR THE 1984 GL1200 CONTINued to cater to customers' concerns for comfort, while the storage compartment in the faux fuel tank maintained a direct link with the original GL.

More changes came in 1983, including cast 11-spoke wheels and Honda's Torque Reactive Anti-Dive Control (TRAC™) system, both carryovers from Honda's racing department. TRAC increases the fork's compression damping under braking, reducing forward pitch and allowing softer suspension rates for better ride quality. Unified braking was also adopted in 1983, which coupled one front disc and the rear brake to operate from the brake pedal, while

the second front disc operated conventionally via the hand lever. Honda's famed RCB endurance road racers debuted a similar system in the early 1980s.

Engineering for comfort reached a higher level in 1983 as well. New suspension provided an even smoother ride, and engine vibration was reduced by gearing that dropped engine rpm at 60 mph from 3400 to 3150. Ergonomically, the Aspencade and Interstate models had their luggage moved rearward to increase passenger room, and adjustable passenger pegs were added as well. Liquid Crystal Diode (LCD) displays also replaced standard instrument dials.

That same year saw Yamaha's introduction of the Venture™, a full-dress touring bike seemingly aimed squarely at the GL's turf. Critics agreed Yamaha's new entry had important strengths, especially in mid-range power, roll-on acceleration and handling prowess. Both critics and worthy competitors are valuable, for they stimulate development. And that's exactly what the Venture did for the Gold Wing, but not the way you might imagine. Honda could have altered the Gold Wing's path to compete directly with the sporty Venture, but instead again listened to its customers, pushing the Gold Wing toward even greater long-distance luxury.

The 1984 GL1200 again revolutionized motorcycle touring. Honda enlarged the same basic powerplant to 1182cc, and increased its punch through larger intake valves and more aggressive cam timing. This brought peak torque 500 rpm earlier in the rev range, and allowed rpm at 60 mph to fall below 3000. The result: The new GL provided greater roll-on performance and at the same time offered the lowest cruising rpm—and subsequently smoothest engine—in the class. The enlarged engine could drive the GL1200 authoritatively even while just loafing along.

Handling was another revolution. As the GL accumulated more luxury items, it also gained more weight. Yet here was a motorcycle that weighed 723.3 pounds (dry), and offered marvelously light steering. Honda's ability to make the Gold Wing feel hundreds of pounds lighter than it was began in earnest with the 1200, and continues to be a hallmark of the Gold Wing today. On the 1200, Honda accomplished this first by making the chassis considerably stiffer, adding bigger fork tubes, and shifting weight

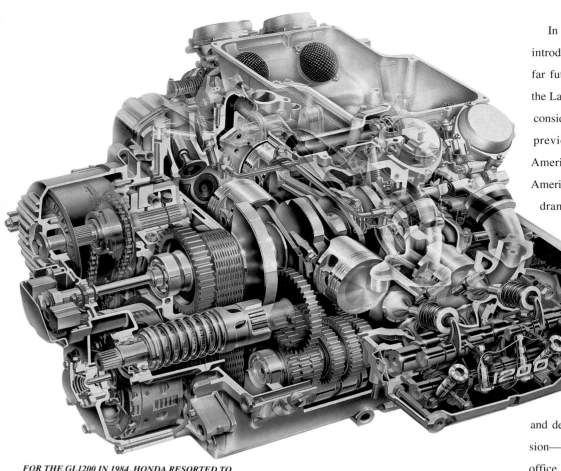

FOR THE GL1200 IN 1984, HONDA RESORTED TO standard hot-rod tuning tactics for more power, including a displacement increase to 1182cc, but also altered final drive gearing for smooth highway cruising.

forward by pushing the engine ahead 2.5 inches. Smaller-diameter wheels—from 18 inches to 16 inches in front, and from 16 inches to 15 inches in back—helped reduce steering resistance. With smaller-diameter wheels placing the GL's seat closer to the ground, Honda engineers were able to increase rear suspension travel a full inch from the 1100's all-time low of 3.1 inches, giving the 1200 a plush ride that once again set the standard for touring machines.

The critics loved it. *Cycle* magazine's GL1200 road test signed off with the words, "This year the Honda engineers have pulled off an unbelievable trick—they've taken a 790-pound [wet] machine and made it nimble and manageable. The choice is clear. Why put up with a big-feeling touring mount when you can have something as close to magic as we've seen in a long time?"

Even while this all-new machine was being readied for market, though, Honda engineers knew that existing trends, continued indefinitely, would make the flat-four engine obsolete. As the cylinders became larger to meet the demands of more power and the engine revved lower to meet vibration requirements, the Gold Wing's power pulses became bigger, spaced further apart. Power delivery was becoming rougher, and any increase in displacement might make vibration unacceptable. Where should the Gold Wing go from here?

In January of 1984—the same year the 1200 was introduced—a new team was assembled to plan the far future of the GL. Shigehisa Morinaka would be the Large Project Leader. One of the first steps was to consider the existing owner surveys and data on the previous models, research largely undertaken by American Honda and Honda Research of America. American involvement in GL development increased dramatically during this period, beginning at the very outset of the project. The bike would undergo its most dramatic transformation yet, and that posed the inevitable question: How far could the GL depart from its existing design before customers rejected it as being a Gold Wing in name only?

In Japan, GL development engineers and designers held a *Y-Gaya*—or brainstorming session—in a small town far from the distractions of the office. American Joe Boyd, a Honda Research development test rider who had earned the nickname GL Joe for his knowledge of and devotion to the Wing, was asked to join the group to provide the customer's viewpoint. "I'll never forget when I walked into the room for the first time," recalls Boyd. "It seemed all the knowledge in the world of motorcycling was there in one room."

A *Y-Gaya* is a no-limits design discussion, illustrated by the kinds of ideas that were discussed. One concept involved a styling treatment that used an unbroken band of light all the way around the motorcycle, with headlight, turn signals, taillights and running lights all emanating from this single light bar. Another involved luggage and trunk lids with pneumatic latches. Air management was a big topic, including the idea of a central air tunnel running from the front of the bike to the rear to provide access to hot and cold air for rider and passenger. From this concept came much of the air-management found on the current Gold Wing, including the fairing heater vents that can divert engine heat to the rider's legs to ward off the cold.

Early design sketches of the new Gold Wing looked remarkably like the final product. But for nearly a year, almost all of the sketches showed a flat-four engine, varying from 1300cc to 1400cc. The engineers, who knew the potential power delivery problems of an even bigger four, wanted as before, in 1972, to build a six. But concern for continuity and product recognition fueled a debate between four or six cylinders that ran the length of 1984. The first mock-up came in early spring of 1985—still with a four-cylinder engine. At the same time, a test unit was quickly concocted out of a GL1200 chassis and the old M1 flat-six engine—astonishingly long-lived usefulness for a prototype—weighing just shy of 720 pounds.

Design goals for this next-generation Wing helped fuel the engine debate. The new machine had to be an improvement over the four-cylinder in every way: extremely quiet, with a silky-smooth power delivery, yet it must produce generous passing and hill-climbing torque at low engine speeds. It had to offer the best possible comfort for the grandest style of touring. Handling should be light and responsive, despite the necessary weight. The machine should have the room and load capacity to carry any combination of passenger and accessories. Still, the styling of this new bike was in the final stages before the engine debate was settled in May of 1985. Management decided on the six largely as a pre-emptive strike, for fear another manufacturer might adopt this rational and attractive design first, and cut deeply into the market the Gold Wing had created.

In design, Honda engineers managed to keep the new engine's length only 2.5 inches greater than the four's, but the plan called for more legroom, not less. To achieve it, the engine was shifted forward 40mm (a little more than 1.5 inches) by adopting a V-shaped radiator to provide front wheel clearance. The wheelbase was simultaneously extended to 66.9 inches, providing room for everything.

Weight was a major worry because the engine's mass, being far forward, could make or break the steering feel. Engineer Keiji Kanbe recalls in his quest for

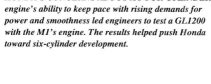

lightness he became slightly overzealous, and crankshafts started breaking on test engines; more material and weight were added until the breakages stopped. The GL1500, as with all Honda engines, was repeatedly tested to destruction to ensure durability at high rpm and high load. Every part that broke was redesigned until it could shrug off such abuse and run full-throttle at the edge of the red zone for 100,000 kilometers.

Makoto Miyake, the fuel system engineer, had to find the best combination of carburetion and manifold for the six. He tested from one to six carburetors on a variety of manifolds. His final choice of two carburetors on a liquid-heated manifold was ideal. (*Cycle* magazine later remarked that the GL's throttle could be opened fully as low as 700 rpm in top gear, and the bike would pull away strongly without hesitation.)

The new engine could dispense with the heavy flywheel used on the fours because its power delivery was naturally smooth. However, the six had strong engine braking once the throttle was closed. The first prototype ridden by American Honda evaluators drew heavy criticism on this point. As one evaluator recalls, "Engine response was almost instantaneous. It was impossible to make smooth shifts. We were really surprised; we expected a six-cylinder engine to have really smooth power delivery. At this point, we began to

HONDA'S CONCERNS ABOUT A FOUR-CYLINDER engine's ability to keep pace with rising demands for power and smoothness led engineers to test a GL1200 with the M1's engine. The results helped push Honda toward six-cylinder development.

HERE'S WHY THE GOLD WING'S cruise control is the standard of the industry: endless hands-on testing, as engineers and test riders strive for perfection.

HONDA MAKES SURE THE SIX-CYLINDER'S combustion does more than merely motivate the bike. A special SE feature, the vent below the valve cover helps route engine-heated air to the rider's feet.

THE SIX SHOWS OFF ITS SOPHISTICATED intake plumbing, with twin computer-controlled carbs, and M1-style coolant-heated manifold.

worry." But the Japanese engineers listened intently to the critique, and set about a solution. A special system—Shot Air™—bypassed fresh air to the intake during deceleration, reducing combustion-chamber vacuum enough to prevent abrupt engine braking.

Chassis problems were tackled as well. With the bigger engine closer to the front, engineers had to deal with increased steering effort. Changing steering geometry to quicker specifications would not compensate unless chassis stiffness was dramatically increased as well. And even here there were obstacles. The flat-six has perfect primary balance, but it retains higher-order

imbalances. The engine designers therefore reasonably wanted to rubber-mount the engine—a first for the Gold Wing. The chassis team, already faced with a need for increased frame stiffness, wanted to use the engine as a major stiffening member, and so lobbied for solid mounting. The need for engine smoothness—again largely customer driven—won out, and the chassis team went back to the drawing boards.

Noise, Vibration and Harshness (NVH) for the 1500 was the province of Osamu Sato, one of the engineers who had so strongly favored rubber engine mounting. His insistence no doubt created headaches for the chassis engineers, but the end result was a machine of unprecedented smoothness. Sato's overall job was to identify every significant sound and vibration source on the machine, and to find ways to keep them from intruding on the rider. Some parts, such as

THESE LIGHTED SWITCHES ON A GL1500 SE control the smoothest, most precise cruise control in motorcycling.

gears, generate sound, while others, such as bodywork panels or crankcase surfaces, may be driven into resonance by sympathetic vibration. As Matsuda had found years ago, one-third of the noise comes from the engine, one-third from the exhaust, and one-third from the chassis itself. One by one, Sato stilled the sources and damped out the resonances.

Another aspect of Sato's work was to tune the 1500's exhaust note. When the CBX came out in 1978, one of its prototype exhausts was tuned to sound like a jet fighter. And for the GL1500, Sato recorded jet exhaust sounds and subjected them to spectrum analysis to discover what combinations of frequencies were perceived by humans as pleasing—and how to make the GL's sound match. This was achieved with a three-section muffler. An emulation chamber reinforces

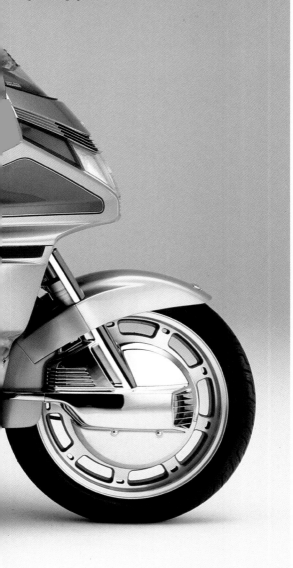

PLANNING FOR THE GL1500 STARTED IN 1984. IN THE ensuing four years before production, Honda built 15 complete bikes that went through 60 prototype stages; a year and a half was spent on frame design alone. One test rider rode prototypes three days a week for two years, and testing consumed some 500 rear tires. The 1991 Gold Wing SE, shown here, features unique two-tone gold paint and graphics.

IT TOOK HONDA MORE THAN A YEAR TO settle the internal six- vs. four-cylinder debate. Once the decision was made, though, the six benefited from Honda's engineering might to become the smoothest, most powerful touring engine extant.

desired frequencies, a resonant absorber tunes out strong unwanted ones, and a dissipative section eats most of the rest.

Meanwhile, the chassis team continued its development with unending chassis and steering geometry changes. Their pursuit of handling perfection was tedious but it got results. Frame designer Shigehisa Morinaka adopted rectangular-section main beams derived from Honda's racing experience, and angled them for the most direct connection between the steering head and swingarm pivot.

A string of test sessions produced round after round of conflicting requests. One rider would ask for more rigidity. Management would see the result was heavier and ask for a different, lighter material. That would drive up cost. At a time when the Japanese yen was rising rapidly against the U.S. dollar, cost increases were unacceptable. It was a delicate balancing act, but ultimately the team created a chassis 1.5 times stiffer than the GL1200—with the desired rubber engine mounts.

It didn't happen overnight. For two and a half years, the GL team followed a formula of setting a performance target, working to reach it, then having management set yet higher targets. The project grew

beyond any before. More than three times the usual number of people were involved in the GL1500 project, working on some 60 prototypes and burning up some 500 rear tires before testing was complete.

Tires were another source of intense development. Honda chose Dunlop to build the tires for the GL, and they would be of bias construction, not radial. Although radial construction was the hot tire trend in 1984, Michelin was the only company with radial experience as the GL1500 project got underway.

Honda knew from owner research that riders liked the fat, cushy look of taller tires, while Michelin's radials—used on Honda racing machines—were very low-profile. Moreover, Dunlop's well-developed U.S. distribution and service network was essential to riders traveling in remote areas of the country.

The target was to produce a tire with all the right handling characteristics that would also deliver a lifespan of 10,000 miles under normal conditions. In a repeating five-month cycle, Honda would propose tire specs, Dunlop would produce test items, Honda would test them, and then again propose altered, higher specs for the next batch. At the peak of development, Dunlop was supplying five different prototype tires a month.

U.S. testing was also far more intense than with any previous model. Normally, new models are tested at three different stages in the U.S., but the Gold Wing was tested more than 20 separate times over the period of a year. A lot of development work went into steering response, with hundreds of suspension and tire combinations explored and tested.

Chief U.S. tester Kioshi Aizawa is credited with pushing the Gold Wing toward perfection, and it was not unusual for U.S. testers to be awakened at 4 a.m. by Aizawa, who wanted to put one of his theories to the test. "He made sure we tested until it just couldn't get any better," recalls Boyd. Much of this testing was done at night in the Arizona desert, in company with a convoy of unmarked support trucks and cars. Secret night touring, anyone?

The Japanese love to measure progress, to quantify research with numerical data. But much of the Gold Wing's development was subjective, impossible to measure. How do you measure seat comfort? Or the way the volume switch detent feels to a gloved hand? Or the level of fatigue felt by a passenger after 10 hours in the saddle? Yet these and other ergonomic qualities were of crucial importance to Gold Wing owners. American riders had become intensely

lowed by a chase van manned by a craftsman from the Tokyo Seat Co. who built new seats on the run, performing endless foam-cutting and hand-stitching in response to rider and passenger comments. U.S. testers spent more time developing the GL1500's seat than on any other single component.

A breakthrough came during one test at 4 a.m. Despite clever layering of foam with various densities, formed into all kinds of contours, there were still lingering discomforts that appeared after hours in the resulting saddles. Testers realized that not only must the seat yield vertically, but its skin must also stretch horizontally as the rider shifted weight or position. They cut the foam surface in a shallow cross-hatch pattern, and the difference in long-term comfort increased dramatically. This cross-hatch method has since been applied to many other Honda models.

The Gold Wing's cruise control system also consumed vast amounts of testing time. Because existing technology—developed for automobiles—provided much too sudden acceleration and deceleration for the Gold Wing, a special R&D program was devised. In the final stages of the work, engineer Yoshiaki Hirakata hunched over an EPROM programmer in the back of a Honda box van, rolling down dark Arizona highways, "burning" new cruise-control chips in response to remarks from test riders. The result is the smoothest, most accurate cruise-control system ever

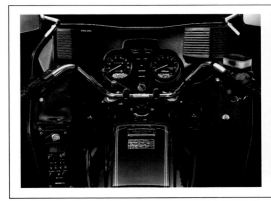  

attuned to these human contact points. Consequently, small details consumed inordinate hours of U.S. development and testing.

Seat design became another major development project. One entire testing session was devoted to developing the 1500's seat, a solid three-week effort of evaluating different combinations of depth, material type, thickness, stiffness, shape, even external stitching methods. Testers had to ride at least 200 miles before even commenting on the saddle, and they were fol-

fitted to a motorcycle.

As with any complex system whose production spans a period of years, the development story of the Honda Gold Wing goes on every day, both in refinements to the existing model, and in as-yet-undisclosed planning and design for future Gold Wings. That process—an ever-closer partnership between Honda and the thousands of GL owners—ensures that the Gold Wing remains the finest expression of the long-distance touring motorcycle.

THREE STAGES IN THE DEVELOPMENT OF the Gold Wing's instruments. The traditional look of analog gauges on the 1980 Interstate gave way to the digital readouts of the Aspencade in 1983. Digital instruments also take center stage on the 1985 GL1200L Limited Edition, joined by a sophisticated trip computer.

A LOWER SEAT HEIGHT IS THE KEY TO the Gold Wing revisions for its 20th anniversary. Lowered suspension and a reshaped and repadded saddle drops the dimension down to 29.1 inches for all three models.

IT COULD HAVE BEEN SO SIMPLE. THE GOLD Wing, one of the most customer-developed vehicles in history, was due for a little tweaking as it approached its 20th anniversary. Some customers had been clamoring for a lower saddle height, something Honda had addressed with the Interstate model since 1991; less padding had reduced the Interstate's seat height to 29.5 inches, compared to the SE's and Aspencade's 30.3 inches. The positive response to the Interstate led Honda to choose a similar direction for all three 1995 Gold Wing 20th Anniversary models. It would have been so easy to just chop some foam out of the saddles, supply suspension components with a touch less travel, pin 20th Anniversary badges on the bodywork, and call them new.

That's not how Honda works. Reducing seat height is risky business: Thinner seats can be less comfortable, and shorter suspension travel can easily sacrifice ride compliance. But such shortcomings would go against the Gold Wing's 20-year history of constant, unrelenting development and improvement. No, the 20th Anniversary Gold Wing had to offer much more.

Instead, engineers took the opportunity to go beyond the surface simplicity of seemingly minor changes to expand the Gold Wing's capabilities, and its potential audience.

Honda did so primarily through rigorous suspension development. All '95 Wings retain the wheel travel of the previous model, but shorter, more lightly preloaded springs at both ends reduce static ride height, and thus seat height. Since the Gold Wing now hunkers down more on its suspension, effective travel is reduced, making the selection of proper damping rates crucial. Joe Boyd of Honda R&D did much of the testing and evaluation for the 20th Anniversary models, and says, "Because the total [effective suspension] stroke is reduced, we had to be more refined with the stroke we had."

As a result, engineers had to pay special attention just to maintain existing standards of ride quality and handling. To up one of those standards without shortchanging the other requires considerably more care, and Honda was especially lavish. As a result, damping rates are substantially firmer (see "High Wing Technology" sidebar for details) for more precise chassis control, yet the Gold Wing retains the legendary suspension compliance that continues to set the industry standard for ride comfort.

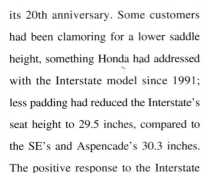

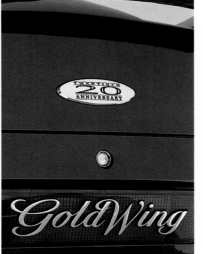

That same care is also evident in how Honda lowered the seat height via the saddle itself. Simply hauling out the electric carving knife and taking a little off the top is a sure ticket to gluteal distress. Instead, Honda constructed a new saddle that's about 0.6 inch lower, but substantially reshaped and recovered. (All three models, Aspencade, SE and Interstate, now share the same saddle.) As Boyd says, "A touring bike is the toughest to make comfortable, because the riding position has you sitting on your hip bones. So the best place to give support is under the thighs. The downside is that's the area you want to take away for easier footing at a stop." Using higher-density foam allowed Honda to reduce seat height, yet reshape the saddle for better support. Another benefit of the shorter seat is that it makes the seat back taller, increasing lumbar support. Honda also added a new seat cover sewn so that it clamshells slightly as you sit in the saddle, further increasing back support.

To make it even easier for riders to get their feet flat and firmly on the pavement, Honda reshaped the GL's sidecovers. Previously convex-shaped, they're

flatter for the 20th Anniversary Wings, and so spread the rider's legs less. And since the bike and rider are lowered by 1.2 inches, the GL gets a correspondingly shorter sidestand, the 0.4-inch-shorter windscreen to match the lower seat, and a handlebar that mounts slightly lower in the triple clamp.

All the changes add up to a motorcycle that feels at once both transformed—and remarkably similar to its taller predecessor. You notice the lowness immediately upon settling into the saddle, especially with the rear air-shock at its recommended minimum load condition of 0 psi. Average-height riders will have a bit of daylight between them and the saddle with their feet planted, and shorter riders will find easier footing aboard 20th Anniversary Wings than on previous models.

Once under way, the Gold Wing seems to feel lighter and smaller, but without losing any of its roominess. At all speeds, it feels more nimble, more athletic, more confidence-inspiring. But where the bike really surprises is on a winding backroad. There, the Gold Wing rides with a newfound composure that thoroughly belies its weight and size—and the seemingly minor changes that netted such dramatic results.

The GL1500 has always had a reputation for superb handling—for an 800-pound motorcycle. With the 20th Anniversary model, Honda has knocked off that last part of the sentence. Lowering both bike and rider has also lowered the GL's center of gravity, making it feel more maneuverable. And with more tightly damped wheel travel, especially at the front, there's less geometry change during

Gold Wing SE

Gold Wing SE

Gold Wing Aspencade

Gold Wing Interstate

NEW COLORS DISTINGUISH THE 20TH ANNIVERSARY Gold Wings, as does special badging on the larger chrome fairing garnish, trunk lid and ignition key. Each bike's combination switch cover also carries a 20th Anniversary emblem with the machine's serial number.

sudden throttle/brake transitions, so the chassis attitude stays more consistent. Both things make the bike feel more composed at all speeds, something any rider can appreciate. And although the suspension is firmer than on last year's Gold Wing, and provides more road feel, ride quality remains excellent, even at the higher rear-shock air pressures required by sport riding or heavy loads.

In fact, all of the things that make the Gold Wing ruler of touring's turf remain present and accounted for in the 20th Anniversary models. The six-cylinder engine retains its status as touring's prime mover; swift, smooth and silent, it can cruise at freeway speeds in relaxed fashion, yet has ample power to pass without downshifting. Single-key remote latches for the trunk and saddlebags keep the Wing in a class of its own for convenient cargo loading. And the AM/FM cassette stereo on the Aspencade and

SE—which moved one writer to say it was "the best thing to happen to outdoor music since Woodstock"—and each model's excellent fairing still keep rider and passenger content until they reach their destination.

Some things, after all, you just don't mess with. But the changes Honda did make reflect some important considerations, and first among them is the Honda Way. You can see it in the continuous *kaizen*—improvement—and response to customer demands that have characterized the GL's history. And you can see it in how Honda chose to answer the need for a lower seat height in a way that broadens the Gold Wing's focus by broadening its function—all without diminishing the bike's legendary luxury. That's been the GL's heritage throughout, and why the 20th Anniversary models are a fitting bookend to the Gold Wing's second decade.

High Wing Technology

AFTER 20 YEARS, STILL PUSHING THE BOUNDARIES.

RIGHT FROM THE START, HONDA'S Gold Wing probed the outer limits of what was possible. Today, the concept of design without limits or limitations, design that pushes the boundaries, has become a Honda hallmark, and can be seen throughout the current generation of Gold Wing GL1500s.

Years of familiarity with the six-cylinder Wing can obscure the importance of its innovations, but it can also illuminate its advantages. It is not uncommon to find well-maintained GL1500s running around with 100,000 or 200,000 miles on the odometer. That kind of durability stems from solid, innovative design.

The liquid-cooled 1520cc sohc engine remains the only six-cylinder motorcycle powerplant in mass production. A horizontally opposed configuration, it offers perfect primary and secondary balance for smoothness, with rubber mounting to quell higher-order vibration. As a six, its power pulses are more evenly spaced than a four's, again for the velvety smoothness crucial to touring comfort. Other benefits cascade from the six's architecture: a low center of gravity for ease of handling, and convenience of packaging for its many subsystems.

So much of a motorcycle's character flows from the engine, and Honda pushed the boundaries of complexity to ensure the six would be as civil as an English butler. Such civility extends largely from extraordinarily tight control of both the fuel/air mixture and its temperature, and of ignition timing. Honda borrowed freely from its automotive technology to accomplish those goals—a first among motorcycles.

The computer-controlled pair of 36mm CV carbs, for example, send mixture through a six-runner manifold which is heated automotive-style with engine coolant to stabilize intake temperatures—a practice dating all the way back to the innovative M1. A Hot Air Intake System also regulates intake air temperature via a bimetallic valve that routes warm air from around the exhaust headers to the airbox. Temperature even regulates the accelerator pump, which pumps at full capacity when the engine is cold for better throttle response, yet cuts flow at higher engine temperatures to help meet EPA emissions regulations.

Automotive-style computer controls further regulate the GL's diet of fuel and air, via sensors that gather information on intake manifold pressure, engine rpm and intake air temperature, among other inputs. In the Primary Main Air Jet Control System, computer-controlled solenoids open or close two jets for optimum air intake. A bellows-type valve in the High Altitude Compensation System uses barometric pressure to vary air intake, increasing flow at higher altitudes and decreasing it at lower ones to maintain crisp throttle response.

Precise control of the ignition spark is also crucial to a broad powerband. The GL utilizes an automotive-style computer-controlled digital ignition, which reads such information as intake manifold pressure and air temperature, plus engine speed and coolant temperature. And, again like Honda's automobile ignition systems, the GL's plots two different and specific advance maps according to gearbox ratio, with one map for first and second gears, and another for third through fifth.

Honda's quest for civility also led to the GL1500's reverse gear system—currently the only mass-produced reverse system in motorcycling—and its extraordinarily accurate cruise control. The reverse gear system became a requirement because the notion of having its customers straining to push the bike out of a parking space was unacceptable to Honda.

The reverse system, however, was never an original component of the GL1500's design, and engineer Kouichi Hikichi had to develop a reverse system in about one-third the normal amount of time. Plus, no other reverse system for motorcycles existed, so there was no standard of performance; Hikichi had to create those standards. It's another example of how Honda pushed the boundaries with the GL.

In operation, pulling up on the reverse lever—with the engine running, but in neutral—locks the gearbox in neutral, and engages a planetary gear which connects the starter to the final drive gear. Punching the starter button then allows the starter to back up the Wing at approximately 1 mph. A host of electronic failsafes defeat the system if the electronics malfunction, the engine stalls, or if the bike tips too far to one side. Also, a speed limiter slows the bike on descents.

Where the Gold Wing's reverse gear had to create new standards, the bike's cruise control took existing ones and elevated them. The system includes the usual resume/accelerate, set/decelerate controls, and is an absolute model of smooth operation. In addition to a particularly sophisticated EPROM chip, the cruise control's precision also stems from using an electronic pickup for the tachometer to read crank speed directly, rather than doing so mechanically via the speedometer cable. During testing of the system, Honda test riders engaged in a friendly competition to make it better than it really needed to be, and their dedication shows.

Similar dedication drove Honda to produce a frame of unusual stiffness for the Gold Wing. Frame rigidity is crucial to the lightness and precision of a motorcycle's steering, and all previous GL engines had been solid-mounted, which contributed greatly to chassis stiffness. But to achieve the desired engine smoothness, the GL1500 powerplant was rubber mounted. Consequently, achieving the additional frame stiffness demanded endless hours of Computer Assisted Design and on-road testing. Engineer Shigehisa Morinaka—in charge of the GL1500's frame—spent an arduous year-and-a-half developing the desired rigidity and handling characteristics.

Other GL1500 chassis features include a unified braking system that actuates the rear and right front brake calipers via the foot pedal while the bar-mounted lever actuates only the left front caliper. Also, on the SE and Aspencade models, an on-board air compressor pressurizes the right rear shock to alter ride height according to load.

The 1995 20th Anniversary models' biggest departures from the previous versions lie in seat height and suspension tuning. The same force that has shaped the Gold Wing since Day One—customer requests—is at work here again, but with a twist. Customers had asked for a lower seat height, and Honda responded, chopping 1.2 inches out of that dimension for the 20th Anniversary SE and Aspencade. At 29.5 inches, the 1994 Interstate already had a 0.8-inch shorter seat than its stablemates. Now all three models share the same 29.1-inch seat height, and the same saddles.

To start, Honda cut down the SE and Aspencade saddles 0.8 inch, installed higher-density foam to compensate, and added more padding under the rider's thighs to better distribute his weight. Plus, the sidecovers are now flatter instead of being convex-shaped, so the rider's legs aren't bowed out as much. To further lower the bike, engineers fitted shorter springs with less preload, reducing the Wing's static ride height. However, total wheel travel remains unchanged. Since the rider sits 1.2 inches lower overall, Honda installed a new windscreen, which is 0.4 inch shorter than the previous screen.

REVAMPED SUSPENSION TUNING FOR THE GL's 20th anniversary has transformed the bike's handling, without sacrificing its legendary ride quality.

That might all sound fairly simple, and if Honda had stopped right there, the changes would have been welcome but unremarkable. There's far more at work here, though, than just reducing the seat height. Using shorter springs with less preload required extensive suspension tuning to achieve the desired ride and handling qualities. Damping rates went up accordingly, though the lighter Interstate, which has different compression damping rates for each fork leg, actually nets a slight overall drop in compression damping. The result is a more agile, more athletic Gold Wing with ride quality that's as comfortable as the previous model's—qualities that expand both the GL's capabilities and its potential audience.

EACH 1995 GL GETS A COMBINATION SWITCH cover with a 20th Anniversary badge and the bike's serial number. A 0.4-inch-lower windscreen complements the rider's lower seating position.

It's yet one more example of how the Gold Wing—after 20 years—continues to push the boundaries of what touring bikes are capable of, and our expectations of them. In that respect, the 20th Anniversary Gold Wings carry on a fine family tradition.

MADE IN AMERICA

TECHNOCRAT'S HEART,

GAMBLER'S SOUL.

BUILDING THE ORIGINAL GOLD WING WAS the sort of high-stakes gamble even the most hardened card players would have shied away from. Honda had indeed bet heavily on the growing sophistication and maturity of American motorcyclists, and had won big.

That was penny-ante poker, though, compared to Honda's gamble to build a motorcycle manufacturing plant in the United States. It wasn't merely a matter of money. The $35 million earmarked for an American motorcycle plant—although hardly chicken feed—would not have crippled the company. But Honda was surely betting the farm: a carefully cultivated reputation for quality, something virtually irrecoverable if the deal went wrong. Honda had earned its place in the American market by building bikes that ran well, were reliable and didn't leak oil—virtues that didn't exist until Honda made them exist.

Honda's plan to manufacture motorcycles in the States set off a firestorm of protest from American Honda staff and dealers in the mid-'70s. Takao Shirokawa, one of the original members of Honda's American plant, remembers, "The U.S. people had the strongest opinion against production in the States." It's easy to see why.

To most consumers, Honda's made-in-Japan quality was its strongest point. And in those days, many American manufacturers' reputation for quality was in free fall, best illustrated by GM's difficulties with the Vega and Ford's with the Pinto. Then there was Harley-Davidson during the turbulent AMF® years, America's only motorcycle manufacturer, whose market share was plummeting due in part to quality problems. These and other examples had raised doubts about the ability of Americans to build anything as complicated as a motorcycle.

Such concerns—and others—raised the stakes even higher for Honda. Plainly, the kind of quality associated with a dollar watch simply would not be tolerated any longer, and a U.S. plant offered the opportunity to change perceptions about American-built quality, an extremely difficult task for attitudes forged in years of disappointment and frustration.

Such a task was vital to Honda's continued success, in part because in the mid-'70s most of Honda's profits came from the American motorcycle market. But, more importantly, if the U.S. plant succeeded, Honda intended to follow it with a $250 million auto plant. Should the motorcycle plant fail—based almost entirely on the quality of the products it produced—the damage to Honda's reputation might have been irreparable, with far-reaching consequences. The motorcycle plant risked everything.

In a sense, building an American plant was inevitable for Honda, a dream of the company's founder and namesake, Soichiro Honda. Too, Honda had an unshakable belief in the importance of building motorcycles in their intended market. With more than 80 percent of Gold Wing production being exported to the United States and Canada after the bike's introduction in 1975, a U.S. plant was vital. Plus, as the most expensive bike in its fleet, the Gold Wing offered the highest potential profit of Honda motorcycles, something the company needed to maintain future development of the U.S. plant. In every sense, the Gold Wing was made for America, and the plant would be made for the Gold Wing.

U.S. production was hardly something Honda rushed into, though. Not that it was a problem of taking production out of Japan, as some might have guessed. Honda had built 30 overseas plants over 25 years, and so had ample experience. But Honda waited to build in America; the market was simply too important to leave to chance. Honda spent more than three years selecting a site for its American plant—roughly the same amount of time it took to develop the very first Gold Wing. After feasibility studies in 1974, organization of a special project for U.S. production started in 1976, which ultimately led to the selection of Marysville, Ohio, a town of 8400 located about an hour's drive from both Columbus and Dayton, for Honda of America Manufacturing (HAM).

Despite Soichiro Honda's assertion that divine providence guided selection of the Marysville site, the selection was also logical. The site nestled right up to

A GOLD WING RAPIDLY TAKES SHAPE ON Marysville's assembly line. Production originally started with CR250s and CBXs in 1979; GLs came on-line May 1, 1980. Currently, Marysville builds 40 to 45 GL1500s daily.

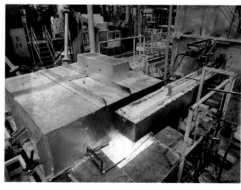

MUCH OF THE GOLD WING IS BIRTHED IN FIRE. Molten aluminum is pressure-fed to dies for crankcases, heads and other parts.

Ohio's Transportation Research Center, with its 7.5-mile test track, one of the best independent tracks in the world at the time, and state-owned. A nearby railroad line and U.S. Route 33 would provide transportation arteries for raw and finished goods. Plus, Ohio ranked third in the nation in number of auto parts suppliers.

Perhaps most important, though, were the people in that somewhat rural area of Ohio. Unemployment then in Ohio ran at more than 10 percent. But what mattered most to Honda was the population's attitude. The region's people descended from American Protestants heavily influenced by Calvinism, with its tenet that hard work and religion were one.

Honda officials visited several manufacturing plants in the Midwest, and became convinced the locals possessed a work ethic similar to that of their Japanese counterparts. That was crucial, because, as Shirokawa says, "Our principal requirement of production was [that] quality should be even higher than products from Japan." That was the only way to preserve Honda's ace in the hole—its reputation.

And Honda went about that task with a unique brand of logic that produced cascading benefits. For instance, a worker's pride goes hand in hand with quality. Quality products preserve the company's reputation, guaranteeing both its position in the marketplace and future expansion, all of which ultimately benefit both the consumer and the worker.

You'll find the same logic in the way Honda built the original 260,000-square-foot Marysville motorcycle plant. Although Honda had 25 years of experience building overseas plants, the Marysville plant was unique because of its small size, so few of the lessons learned at other plants, or in Japan, transferred easily. Japanese plants, in particular, were of little use as a model, in part because of their vastly greater production capacity, and because of their hodgepodge nature; they had been built and then expanded repeatedly over the years. Conversely, many of the key techniques and ideas used in Ohio are not used in Japan.

What Marysville required was strict efficiency. As Shirokawa says, the plant was designed "to minimize traffic between adjacent departments, to try to minimize space, and try to maintain very efficient logistics inside the plant. We tried to make the most efficient, but small, motorcycle plant. Profitability was the key to this plant. So [the question was] how to minimize cost of production. We tried to pursue efficiency of production."

Physically, there was very little about Marysville that broke new ground. For equipment and production, the plant simply relied upon state-of-the-art solutions, the latest in engineering and production techniques. And that included air conditioning, already in use in Japanese plants, but an unheard-of feature in the United States in an era when many factories were dark, dimly lighted environments.

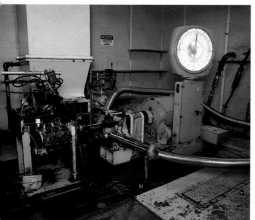

GOLD WING ENGINES ARE PULLED FROM inventory at regular intervals and run on the dyno in Marysville as part of a rigorous quality-control program. Testing is brutal, failures incredibly rare.

Like most of the Marysville facility, though, air conditioning had a far-reaching logic. Air conditioning means good working conditions, both for people and products. It also allowed Honda to provide associates with uniforms, because, as Shirokawa says, "If [the] production area is not air-conditioned, people wear what they need to adjust to temperatures." And the uniforms, of course, were specially designed to have no exposed buttons or zippers, no hard parts that might scratch or damage delicate finishes—further evidence of Honda's deep devotion to quality.

That devotion extends to other extremes. For example, there's Honda's use of its own machinery for production. Inside the Marysville plant, you'll see the usual array of Japanese die-cast machines and American tubing-benders, but most of the precision machining equipment comes from Honda Engineering. In fact, Honda Engineering of Japan built many of the machines used for Gold Wing production, including welding and assembly equipment, dies and molds for fenders and fairings, and fine boring machines for precise machining of the steering head and engine mounts.

AT THE END OF THE PRODUCTION LINE, A 20TH Anniversary Gold Wing gets a final shakedown. A computerized testing program checks a variety of operations.

Quality control is the main reason Honda produces

its own machines to its own exacting standards, but look closer and you'll see a deeper logic. Building machines to make machines provides Honda with a rapid response time; in a competitive market with frequent major model changes, the ability to respond quickly becomes a crucial marketing edge. At Honda Engineering—including Honda Engineering of North America, Inc.—engineers work closely and early in the design process with those in R&D, and so save time in creating new jigs and fixtures for production. The arrangement also allows better, more rapid maintenance, and also upgrading and *kaizen*—improvement, in Japanese—of production equipment and processes.

As the factory itself was being built, Honda set about hiring and training a work force. Initially, HAM employed only 64 associates (as Honda calls its employees), including 10 Japanese staff members, but some 2000 to 3000 people applied. That was surprising enough, since Honda initially hired only people who lived within a 15-mile radius of Marysville, stemming from company policy to hire local area people, so that the community benefits from Honda involvement. (The radius was extended years later and eventually eliminated.) After the selection process, training began, with many of the associates being sent to Japan to get instruction in the assembly process, painting, and welding.

Welding was especially important. Even though the plant was always intended to produce Gold Wings, the first one didn't come off the line until May 1, 1980, almost a year after the factory started production. By 1978, the popularity of aftermarket fairings forced Honda's hand to develop the Interstate, the first Gold Wing equipped with fairing and saddlebags. Such major model changes postponed GL production in Marysville by one year. Meanwhile, HAM produced CR250 motocross bikes, and the special steels and thin-wall tubing for their frames made them difficult to weld—especially for the nine welding associates. Only one had any such experience, and that at welding submarine hulls in an East Coast Navy shipyard. So Honda shipped all nine associates off to Japan to teach them, as Shirokawa puts it, "very basic, but very accurate skills."

Not all associates got such training in Japan, but many did, including those from the paint shop and assembly areas. Steve Yoder's experience was typical. One of the first 14 associates on the assembly line

GL1500 ENGINES COME TO LIFE ON THE ZERO
Line, the original assembly line at the Anna Engine
Plant, and the only one of its kind in the world that pro-
duces both motorcycle and car engines.

in 1979, Yoder has stayed with HAM and is now a senior manager. In 1980, he was sent to Japan with three other production associates to learn the complete Gold Wing production process. They spent three weeks there, eight to 12 hours a day, going over each process, from assembly to tooling to quality control. He was then responsible for coming back and setting up the production line and teaching other associates how to perform their jobs.

Yoder's experience in Japan also shows how eagerly Honda listens to its associates, and how willing the company is to make changes in the production process. Yoder had to bring a gang of wiring through to a box in the front of the bike—a seemingly simple process, except the size of the box's hole was too small. Cycle time on the line for the procedure was 90 seconds; it took him two minutes. He tried to explain it to the production people in Japan. They referred him straight to the bike's designer. Yoder explained the problem, and asked him, "Please show me." Yoder timed him with a stopwatch, and at 90 seconds he said, "The production line has stopped." At two minutes the designer stood up and said, "I under-stand." And the problem got fixed.

Such open communication is encouraged at Honda, and the company takes measures to ensure an equal voice among all associates. Every associate is treated equally, down to the seemingly minor detail of all employees sharing a single, common lunchroom, rather than segregating them into labor and manage-ment dining areas. Honda offers one pay scale for all

assembly workers, which facilitates movement from place to place in the assembly process. This move-ment allows crosstraining of associates, the develop-ment of new skills, and a clearer vision of the entire production process. This kind of involvement has led to many associate-driven improvements to the produc-tion process over the years.

Such crosstraining has long been standard proce-dure at Honda, but was unheard of in 1979, and the multiple pay scales used at most other manufacturing plants, as well as United Auto Worker rules, make it difficult to implement elsewhere. Even today there is no UAW union at HAM, by employee choice. GM's Saturn® plant in Spring Hill, TN, however, is one American manufacturing facility making use of the techniques Honda pioneered in Marysville, discarding some of Detroit's traditional distinctions between labor and management. To create its best-selling Taurus, Ford also employed certain Japanese tech-niques, such as pulling together representatives from all parts of the company to build the new model from scratch, and involving outside suppliers in the process from the start. Honda even conducted a tour of the Marysville plant for a group of Harley-Davidson executives, including then-CEO Vaughn Beals, the year before H-D's buyout from AMF.

It's that human touch—bringing employees closer to the process, rather than rigidly compartmentalizing them, and distancing them from the process and the product—that helps distinguish Honda. And it's also why you'll see fewer robots than you might think at

ANOTHER EXAMPLE OF THE HUMAN TOUCH, using people where you might expect robots. The quality of GL painted parts is higher than that for Honda automobiles, ensured by naked-eye inspection. Paint-shop capacity is the limiting factor in GL production, even running three shifts.

TO HELP ENSURE QUALITY, HONDA BUILDS many of the machines that build the motorcycles. Building its own manufacturing equipment shortens lead time, simplifies maintenance and allows rapid improvements.

such a state-of-the-art production facility as Marysville. But according to Shirokawa, "The assembly area is [the] most difficult area to introduce robots. In [the] case of the auto plant, every 60 seconds, one car passes its process. But in [the] case of the motorcycle plant, the time is more than two minutes, sometimes three minutes. It's very difficult to teach all these processes in one robot." Instead, Honda relies on robots for carrying heavy parts, and in areas where there might be some danger to associates. "We try to improve working circumstances by introducing robots," Shirokawa says.

Parts supply offers yet another telling insight into the Honda Way, a way of doing things that produces multiple benefits. Not everyone was willing to step up and take the gamble with Honda—at least not initially. As Shirokawa says, "The hardest part of opening the Ohio plant was finding suppliers who both wanted to supply parts, and were able to supply quality parts for a low price. Before we started producing motorcycles [in Ohio], no suppliers were interested in supplying parts to Honda, because the production capacity was too small."

Small, indeed. For instance, on September 10, 1979, for the first day of the Marysville production, associates cranked out 10 CR250s; through 1981 to 1983, maximum daily production of Gold Wings was 150. By comparison, in 1975, one of Honda's Japanese plants churned out 1000 to 2000 units daily. With Marysville's low numbers, and Honda's rigid quality requirements, it's easy to see why, as Shirokawa says, "Local parts supply started with fighting." Honda started hunting for suppliers three years before the Marysville plant even opened—again, about the same amount of time it took to develop the original Gold Wing.

Some of the original suppliers had been providing parts to Detroit's automakers, and were neither used to the level of quality Honda demanded, nor willing—initially—to make the expensive changes in production necessary to provide such high quality in such low volume. Honda worked extremely closely with its vendors, offering training, advice and even furnishing production equipment—an unheard-of relationship between client and vendor at the time, and still rare in this country. Most suppliers appreciated Honda's involvement, because it allowed them to improve their quality, and thus expand their business.

The story of Dick Taylor's Taylor Metals, one of HAM's first vendors, is typical. Taylor Metals supplied mufflers for the Gold Wing—and still does—but the emphasis on quality, especially in appearance, made the task difficult at first. Honda sent people to assist Taylor and suggest changes, Dick Taylor says, "for quite awhile, until they were sure you were at their level of quality. Many times they questioned your ability to provide parts at their level of quality." Asked if it was difficult or frustrating to achieve Honda's level of quality, Taylor says, "Oh, yes. [But] they were always willing to send people to help out. They were truly a partner in the original production." Honda even furnished some of the machinery for Taylor's plant to produce GL parts. When asked what he and his firm had to do differently, Taylor says, "Nothing, really. The things we probably didn't do methodically, they were very insistent on doing that way. With Honda, you don't bend the line. You just go straight. We as Americans tend to go one way or the other, to expedite things. They don't do that; they go in a straight line."

The same concern for quality that drove production of the first GL in Marysville is evident today, and it reaches well beyond machines. It's a human touch, trained eyes that search a Gold Wing's painted surfaces for imperfections, checking the gloss and smoothness against a master test piece, to ensure a higher standard of finish than even for the Accord and Civic automobiles produced next door in the Marysville auto plant. As Shirokawa says, "Naked eye quality inspection is the key."

Gold Wings also exceed Honda auto standards in tightness of tolerances held on their crankshaft main bearings front to rear, as part of a larger regimen to reduce noise and increase smoothness. On a motorcycle—unlike a car—you sit directly above the engine, listening to every little sound it makes. Other examples of unusually high quality standards abound in Marysville. How do Gold Wings maintain such precise fit and finish? Brackets that hold bodywork are held to tight tolerances, then finish-machined for near-perfect alignment, an extremely unusual practice for motorcycle—or automobile—production. Tight control of mold temperature, cure time and paint temperature for plastic body parts also yields increased precision, as does the use of virgin plastics. These are all extreme measures for motorcycle production, but serve to underscore the long-term quality of the venerable Gold Wing.

Such quality was something Honda never gambled

on. The company's unswerving devotion to that con-cept—every step of the way—started long ago, and continued right from the beginning at Marysville. Within three months of startup in Ohio, Honda's top managers had sufficient confidence in HAM's quality to go ahead with building the auto plant in 1979—the first Japanese car builder to do so in the U.S. Expansion of the auto plant followed in 1984, accom-panied by the decision to build an engine plant in nearby Anna, to produce engines both for cars and the Gold Wing. Anna expansion followed in 1987, as did another auto plant in East Liberty, Ohio. Since the Marysville startup, Honda has made a total capital investment of $2.8 billion there, and employs a work-force more than 10,000 strong.

The Gold Wing was there at the beginning, a piv-otal chapter in Honda's American success story. To build one of its most important, enduring motorcy-cles, Honda built the most important plant in its histo-ry, and hedged its bet on an enduring virtue: Quality.

BUILDING MOTORS IN THE HEARTLAND

HAM GOES AEP

Just outside the little Midwestern town of Anna, Ohio, some 40 miles up the road from Marysville, you can see how broad Honda's definition of Made In America becomes. It's at the Anna Engine Plant (AEP) where Honda builds *engines,* the things that gave purpose and passion to Soichiro Honda in his youth.

Like the Marysville plant, Anna was built for the Gold Wing, further evi-dence of the GL's wide-ranging influence on Honda. And, just as Marysville's success paved the way for Honda's auto manufacturing efforts in this country, so did Anna, moving from producing GL engines alone to building powerplants for Civics and Accords, automatic transmissions and suspension components. At Anna, all the casting, forging, machining and heat-treating processes necessary to turn raw materials into finished, sophis-ticated engines reside under one roof. As one insider said, "We do what seven Honda plants do in Japan."

Designed in Japan and set up there before being shipped piecemeal to America, the original 192,000-square-foot Anna facility opened on July 22, 1985. Before that, though, a core group of associates, hand-picked from the Marysville plant, traveled to Japan and spent 10 hours a day for six weeks learning the GL engine-building process. Back in Anna, a group of five American associates, with some Japanese help, spent two-and-a-half weeks, eight hours a day building Gold Wing engines and tearing them down, hon-ing their skills and preparing for production. After the plant's opening, the five Americans assembled all the Gold Wing engines, with each associate building a complete engine, following it around the conveyor, doing what is now the job of six associates. The five did their job on Zero Line, the origi-nal assembly line at Anna. This line, later expanded to incorporate Civic and Accord engine assembly, is the only one of its kind in the world to produce both motorcycle and car engines.

Although HAM had the tooling to begin production of another motorcycle engine—for the VT1100C Shadow—by 1986, the decision was made to start Civic engine production, and with it came the end of one-associate/one-engine assembly. Shortly after Civic production began, HAM embarked on a $450-million, 650,000-square-foot expansion at Anna to accommodate pro-duction of Accord engines, automatic transmissions (assembled in a pressur-ized clean room), and suspension and brake components. Said to be the most highly integrated engine and drivetrain production facility in North America—and operating with one of the highest levels of automation of any auto engine plant on the continent (48 percent of the operations are automat-ed)—the 1.2-million-square-foot facility can make, from scratch, some half a million engines a year. That's 2100 per day, or one about every 27 seconds.

Honda builds Gold Wing engines at Anna in the early morning, at the beginning of the first shift. That seems only fitting, because at Anna, the Gold Wing started it all.

HONDA HISTORY

IN A LAND THAT VALUES CONFORMITY AND ACADEMIC
THINKING, SOICHIRO HONDA WAS A MAVERICK. WITHOUT HIM,
THE STORY OF HONDA WOULD BE A BLANK PAGE.

HONDA MOTOR COMPANY was created by one man, Soichiro Honda, in a human lifetime. At a time when corporations tend to be faceless entities, Honda Motor Company stands out as the expression of one man's personality, of his engineering knowledge and energy. Yes, Honda has policies, offices and factories like other corporations, but it also continues to reflect the maverick personality of its creator.

"The Old Man," as he was affectionately known, died in 1991 at the age of 84, 43 years after forming the Honda Motor Company on an investment of $3200. But he left an indelible mark on his company, a way of doing business that became uniquely the Honda Way.

He seemed to be everywhere and he remembered everything. Before his retirement in 1973, he went from department to department every working day, checking on progress, suggesting alternatives, making engineering the central preoccupation of his company and his people. This hands-on philosophy is at the root of the many innovations Honda has produced over the years, a philosophy that started at the top. Mr. Honda himself produced more than 470 patented designs during his career.

Because Soichiro Honda saw everything that went on in his company, he was in a unique position to blend ideas and technologies from apparently unrelated areas, into new solutions that might not have occurred to pure specialists, isolated in remote departments. It is a philosophy that continues at Honda today.

Mr. Honda also urged all his people to accept mistakes as the price of learning, not as the disgrace of failure. Engineering is taught as a near-exact science of mathematical relationships and physical properties, but in actual practice it is far less well-defined. Prototypes embodying new ideas must be built, tested, talked over, improved, and tested again. Most will be rejected—but they are not therefore failures. They are steps from ignorance toward knowledge, brush strokes that sketch out new directions, new areas of work. Work, fail, learn, and work again.

This Honda Way of development has always driven the company to explore new ideas and new directions without fear of failure. Indeed, Honda has always preferred to take the risk of failing to achieve progress. The process was not always painless, however. According to Robert L. Shook's "Honda: An American Success Story," a burned piston cost Honda the race at a 1965 British road race Grand Prix. Mr. Honda personally supervised the engine's teardown, and demanded to know who designed the piston. A young engineer named Shoichiro Irimajiri stepped forward to confess. Irimajiri would become the architect of Honda's five- and six-cylinder GP bikes of the '60s, the designer of the six-cylinder CBX, Large Project Leader of the M1, and president of Honda of America Manufacturing.

"Why did you make these changes?" Mr. Honda demanded. Irimajiri confidently explained his theory to him, and Mr. Honda exploded. "Who do you think you are talking to? I designed and made that! I have been making and working with pistons for more than 20 years. If you think college academics is everything, you are totally wrong."

With that, Mr. Honda told Irimajiri to take the

SOICHIRO HONDA, LEFT, AND TAKEO FUJISAWA.
Fujisawa joined Honda Motor Company as managing director in 1949. The two were very close, and retired together in 1973.

TWO THINGS THAT RADICALLY ALTERED FOR-
ever how Americans viewed motorcycles: the "You Meet the Nicest People on a Honda" ad, and the Hondells, with their tune "Little Honda." The song made the Top Ten in 1964, and was later covered by the Beach Boys.

offending piston to each person in the machining and casting shops who had worked on it and apologize for his mistake. Adding further embarrassment, Mr. Honda followed Irimajiri as he made the rounds.

The same anecdote also illustrates another element of the Honda Way. Mr. Honda did not believe in walls—either of the physical variety that separate departments, or of the intellectual variety that forbid one branch of engineering to interest itself in another. Another wall Honda did not respect was the wall of professionalism that in other companies keeps practical men out and lets in only those who scored high on university exams. Promotion at Honda depended upon ability to solve problems—not upon academic status.

Takeo Fujisawa joined Honda in 1949, and is considered a co-founder of the company. He possessed a flair for marketing, and shared Honda's vision and love of things mechanical. Everyone has heard the stories of how Honda, as a boy, chased after the first motorcar that came to his village, breathing in the smell of its exhaust, dipping his fingers into the hot, black oil that dripped from it. This new monster spelled power, a way to leap out of the ordinary world, a way to command nature.

By fortunate physical intuition and a willingness to do the work necessary, he shed the rural heritage of his village to become a master mechanic. During World War II, he tried to manufacture piston rings for aircraft engines, but discovered that his intuition and experience would take him only part-way to a successful product. He therefore returned to school part-time, and spent the rest of his hours scouring libraries for metallurgical information, pestering his instructors, and working to perfect his piston rings. In succeeding, he learned that formal knowledge, applied systematically as research and development, had to sup-

plement raw drive and intuition.

When, after the war, he switched to the manufacture of clip-on motorbike engines, he continued the method, and it worked. Competing transportation products were distributed locally, their parts often made by hand and far from interchangeable. Honda produced machines that worked well, and could be easily repaired using common tools. He knew that semi-handmade motorbikes that could only be repaired by those who had built them would never have wide use.

Mr. Honda was not afraid of defeat, for he had discovered a method that used defeat as a steppingstone to success. When he traveled to Europe in 1954, he saw that European motorcycles were far ahead of the best that his company could then produce. He bought examples of European parts and returned to Japan to show his engineers what their competitors could do. He also placed a large order for advanced types of European machine tools, able to work to closer tolerances, at higher speeds than current Japanese tooling. Each time a department needed specialized equipment for research, the answer was, "Order it."

In 1955, Honda began its long career in racing, designing a four-cylinder 250cc racer that nearly equaled the power level of its European competition. In seven years of hard development, Honda would win the World Championship with the descendants of that 250. Meanwhile, Honda built its first overhead cam production bike—the 11 horsepower Dream SA. Two years later came a crucial departure from the conventional—the electric-starting 250cc C70. At a stroke, this machine made motorcycling immensely more attractive to millions of potential riders. Serious income for basic research was provided by exploding sales of the Super Cub 50 step-through, beginning in 1958.

Mr. Honda was already looking beyond Japan, to more prosperous nations in which motorcyclists could afford more than the bare minimum vehicle. There was an opportunity here. Yet the Cub was extremely important, for it earned a profit despite the transportation industry's belief that small vehicles equaled small profits. Honda had mastered a difficult problem—and would now elaborate the method to more and more complex machines.

Honda set about enlarging the appeal of its products. The 125cc Benly twin of 1959 showed the company could produce a European-style sports machine of small displacement and good performance. In 1960 came the

Hawk® and Super Hawk sports models, with performance comparable to well-established machines such as the Triumph 500, and with something far more important: electric starting, plus automobile-like reliability. In a time when European bikes needed frequent maintenance, and their factories expected all owners to be mechanics, Honda machines were turn-key transportation for anyone who wanted it.

In the United States, the Super Cub and subsequent small Hondas had been deliberately marketed as being cute and harmless, in strong contrast to the big bikes then so popularly associated with "social undesirables." These little machines were reliable and durable, earning a strong reputation for their maker. Indeed, the very name, Honda, was used by many as a generic term for any small motorcycle. The brilliant advertising campaign that proclaimed "You Meet the Nicest People on a Honda," countered the social stereotype of motorcyclists, and helped put thousands of Americans on Super Cubs and other little Hondas. Many of these buyers soon sought something a little bigger—and then something bigger yet. Step by little step, Honda created the market for motorcycles in this country, and supplied it.

Why was this not done first by one of the established, experienced European or British makers? The answer is in production, another example of the Honda Way. Every Honda product was designed, right from the outset, not only to do the job intended, but also to be

quickly and easily produced. For example, Honda engines were built on horizontally split crankcases, allowing crank, gearbox, and accessory drives to be set into one case half, one part at a time. When the cases were closed and bolted up, assembly was complete—there were no time-consuming press-fits, bearing shimming or finicky adjustments to make. Design for production made it possible to build these machines on a simple production line, without fancy skills or equipment, which, by cutting production cost and time, priced Honda machines where millions could afford them.

THAT WAS THEN; THIS IS NOW: AT TOP IS THE official company truck outside American Honda Motor Co., Inc. headquarters on Pico Boulevard in Los Angeles, 1959. Above is an aerial view of what was to come, American Honda Motor Co., Inc., North American headquarters, and Honda Research and Development in Torrance, California.

The aspect of Honda's success that was most puzzling to Europeans was the company's ability to put complex features such as overhead cams and electric starting into competitively priced machines. Using European design and manufacturing practice, such features would have been impossible, for everything added would require more handwork and more time. But each time Honda engineers added a new feature, they also simplified its implementation. The first single-overhead-cam Hondas had ball cam bearings, but when double overhead cams were used on the CB450 twin, the bearings were simplified to plain bushings. Later

THREE DIFFERENT EXAMPLES OF HONDA'S visions: the 1970 CB750 (left), the mighty six-cylinder CBX of 1979 (center), and the 1967 CL77 Scrambler 305.

HONDA WAS ALWAYS SEARCHING FOR NEW avenues of power. One of them was oval pistons for increased valve area, as illustrated here in the 1992 NR750.

still, cams would run directly in the aluminum cylinder heads. When Honda doubled apparent complexity by creating the first mass-production four-cylinder, the CB750, the engineers simultaneously simplified its design by adopting an automotive-style forged one-piece crank, turning in plain bearings. Had this crank used the ball and roller bearings of its predecessor twins, it would have required a minimum of eight-piece construction, all precisely pressed together and aligned. In this way, each improvement in function was accompanied by production simplifications that made the improvement economically possible. Products of higher function were delivered to the public at competitive prices.

Honda engineers also knew and understood complexity. During the 1960s, when Honda racing machines won the first of their many World Championships, it was with tiny, high-revving twins, fours, fives, and sixes with tiny, jewel-like valves, pistons and other moving parts. All the crankshafts in these machines had been of the roller bearing, multi-element type, requiring press-fit assembly and alignment by highly skilled craftsmen. Engineers knew the immense cost of this kind of construction, and they knew it could never find a mass market. By mastering the traditional ways to achieve high performance, Honda engineers learned what was essential and what was not, and then found ways to deliver similar high performance from simplified designs that could be produced at reasonable cost. In 1963, it was considered

MR. HONDA RECEIVED WORLDWIDE RECOGNITION FOR his many accomplishments when he was inducted into the Automotive Hall of Fame in Detroit in 1989.

fantastic to field a factory-racing 250cc four-cylinder, turning 14,500 rpm. Honda now routinely produces street motorcycles that spin this high.

Racing success provided many benefits to Honda. It helped make the company name a worldwide household word. It decisively proved that Japan was capable of innovation—something that many were eager to deny. It provided Honda's engineers with tough, real problems whose solutions showed the way to better products.

In the mid-1960s Honda began to produce automo-

emerge from this work.

During the years of intensive automotive development, 1968-76, Honda temporarily withdrew from motorcycle GP racing to focus on booming market demands. A wave of new models began in 1978 and 1979, including the six-cylinder CBX. Simultaneously, the company accelerated work on new kinds of four-stroke racing engines, including the legendary V-4 oval-piston NR500, a technological marvel that helped usher in a new era of successful V-4 production models, beginning with the Sabre and Magna, then continuing with the sporting Interceptors of 1983 and 1986, through the classic RC30 and RC45 sportbikes. Honda has gone on to win numerous 500cc and 250cc world titles in GP road racing, using two-stroke powerplants evolved from the company's long-successful motocross racing program. As before in the 1960s, tackling the problems of GP racing generated a fresh current of technology with widespread applications.

Soichiro Honda retired from active leadership in 1973 but remained a familiar figure in every department for many years thereafter. He is remembered as a no-nonsense practical man, an entrepreneurial spirit who had shown that a single person can still make a difference in the era of corporations. He had spent his life with his engineers and technicians, suggesting, cajoling, pushing against accepted boundaries and inspiring those around him to do the same.

biles, at first small sports designs with motorcycle-like engines. Simultaneously, the company entered Formula One auto racing, also using a motorcycle-like engine design. Neither effort was a great success, but the company pushed ahead, working hard to master technologies essential in automotive engineering. From this work came the Honda CVCC low-emissions engine in the Civic automobile introduced in 1975, proving that Honda had reached world class in auto design. In the 1980s, turbocharged Honda F1 racing engines would dominate auto GPs, and continued to expose Honda engineers to work on the leading edge of technology.

Honda combined its automotive design practice with existing motorcycle design and production. The CB750 four was an early product of this synthesis, but the most definitive was the Gold Wing. It joined the automotive virtues of smooth operation, long life, and low maintenance to the traditional attraction and excitement of the motorcycle.

In the early 1970s, off-road motorcycling became popular in the U.S., and Honda worked to master the special problems of off-road suspension. Not only were Honda off-road machines successful, but their development yielded important new understandings of fork and damper technology that were soon applied to all Honda machines. Long-travel suspension, gas-pressurized dampers, large-diameter low-friction fork assemblies, and the use of aluminum as a frame material would all

THE HUMAN TOUCH

TRACING TWO DECADES OF GL TECHNICAL
DEVELOPMENT CHARACTERIZED BY
ENGINEERING FOR HUMAN CONCERNS.

A RIVER OF TECHNOLOGY RUNS THROUGH motorcycling, one hip-deep in engineering solutions to engineering problems. Most often, the overriding goal is ever-higher performance. Gold Wing development, however, has carved out a unique tributary. Just as the singular demands of long-distance touring forced Honda to define new objectives to create the Gold Wing, so did engineers have to adopt a whole new way of thinking to address the GL's primary goal: unparalleled long-term touring comfort.

Long-distance comfort, at best a subjective goal, is difficult to pin down. How do you accurately measure a seat's comfort, or the serenity of a cockpit on a 400-mile day? How do you compensate for the differences in human characteristics? Engineering for performance is fairly straightforward: Faster is better. But comfort?

Touring carries its own unique concerns, and tour-

ing riders are quite vocal about their likes and dislikes. As a result, for 20 years the GL has marched in lock step to the desires and objections of its owners. The GL created touring as we know it, but, like a smoothly polished river stone, both the bike and the market have been shaped by customers over the years. This relentless program of development also contributed to the concept of continuous improvement, a concept driven by continuous, active dialogue with owners that has since become an industry-wide tool for making products embody what owners expect of them.

Such customer-driven development established several clearly defined trends during the Gold Wing's life. And one of the first things customers asked for was more top-gear roll-on power—the ability to pass traffic at highway speeds with nothing more than a flick of the right wrist. Downshifting was undesirable.

The first GL1000's shortage of roll-on punch reflected Honda's less-than-crystal-clear focus on what the bike should have been. Although engineers wanted the GL tuned for maximum torque and a broad power-band, Honda management also knew what worked in the marketplace in the mid-'70s: peak performance. As a result, that first GL was second only to Kawasaki's Z-1 in quarter-mile acceleration, and its torque peak came at a high, 6500 rpm, far from the engine's speed—3500 rpm—at 60 mph in top gear.

There are two ways to improve roll-on performance. A quick fix is to regear the engine to spin faster, bringing roll-on rpm up closer to peak torque rpm. But this easy approach trades one problem for another. Spinning the engine faster increases both vibration and noise. Vibratory forces rise with the square of speed: Double the rpm, get four times the shaking. A better solution is to spread the power, shifting the torque peak down to coincide with the engine's rpm at 60 mph. And that's precisely what Honda did to the Gold Wing's engine for 1978. Smaller carburetors and shorter cam timing improved cylinder filling in the low-rpm range, while more ignition advance helped increase torque.

Honda approached these changes with caution

because, while they indeed boosted low-end performance, they also robbed the GL of some of its top-end sting. It was difficult for Honda to accept the notion that its customers were willing to trade top-end for roll-on acceleration; you can see the effect of the changes on the GL's top-end power by the 1978 model's slower quarter-mile time. *Cycle* magazine published a time of 12.92 seconds at 104.52 mph for the original GL in 1975, and 13.38 seconds at 98.90 mph for the 1978 version.

Boosting roll-on acceleration is more easily accomplished with increased displacement, and that's the path Honda chose for the Gold Wing's first major redesign in 1980, bumping displacement to 1085cc. Engineers reconfigured the cylinder heads for better combustion at low and middle rpm; to boost torque further they increased valve lift slightly, lengthened cam duration, reduced carb size another millimeter (to 30mm, from the '78's 31mm and the original's 32mm), and added a magnetically triggered ignition with vacuum advance for more precise spark control. Engineers also shortened gearing slightly to bring engine rpm and peak torque rpm closer together at 60 mph. This shorter gearing made the 1980's engine rpm at 60 mph—3700—the highest of the entire GL

GOLD WING CRANKSHAFTS—SUCH AS THE ONE for a GL1500 seen here—are created to exceptionally close tolerances, and bearing tolerances are even closer than those for Honda automobiles. Such attention to detail makes the engine smoother and quieter.

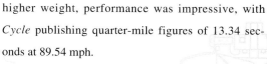

SMOOTH AND SILENT, THE FIRST GOLD WING engine was a revelation at the time, with the quieting effects of its automotive-influenced liquid cooling, belt cam drive and shaft final-drive.

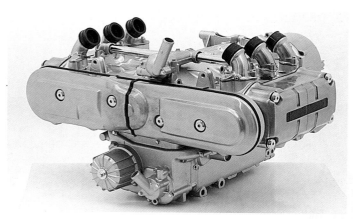

THIS WOODEN MOCK-UP FOR THE GL1500 SIX-cylinder engine dates back to the mid-'80s, yet shows its unmistakable Gold Wing heritage—including individual intake manifolds for six separate carbs.

family, but it also—in conjunction with the displacement increase and tuning changes—helped make the 1980 GL1100 standard the quickest member of the GL family, posting a quarter-mile time of 12.47 seconds at 107.39 mph (*Cycle* magazine).

The 1980 model showed how Honda juggled the conflicting demands of roll-on power and noise and vibration control—and continued to do so year after year with different solutions. Engineers especially fussed over the Gold Wing's overall gearing, searching for the right combination. For 1982, the GL received taller ratios for third, fourth and fifth gears to lower cruising rpm; for the 1983 model, Honda fitted taller primary drive ratios for even taller overall gearing. The result made for more relaxed engine speeds at 60 mph, dropping engine rpm from the highest 1980 figure of 3700 rpm to 3390 for 1982, and to 3144 for 1983. It also made the 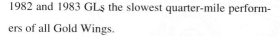 1982 and 1983 GLs the slowest quarter-mile performers of all Gold Wings.

The appearance of Yamaha's Venture in 1983, with its good roll-on power and capable handling, makes it easy to assume Honda responded with the Gold Wing's next major makeover for 1984. But the development team for the 1984 GL1200 was selected in the spring of 1982; they already knew what they wanted, and what had to be done.

They began with more displacement, this time 1182cc, accompanied by longer cam duration, more valve lift, more squish area in the combustion chambers, and bigger carbs, back to the original's 32mm throat size. As before, most of these changes were aimed at boosting midrange, but Honda obviously wanted to keep some top-end power as well. New final drive gearing produced the tallest overall gearing yet for the GL. Engine redline dropped to 7500 rpm—a whopping 2000 rpm down from the 1975 model's figure—with engine rpm at 60 at an all-time low of 2977 rpm. Despite the tall gearing and

higher weight, performance was impressive, with *Cycle* publishing quarter-mile figures of 13.34 seconds at 89.54 mph.

Performance took a big jump for 1985, with the GL1200 Limited Edition, which benefited from shorter overall gearing and fuel injection, for quarter-mile figures of 12.88 seconds at 102.32 mph. Again Honda had shortened primary gearing, but fitted a taller gearbox ratio for fifth, so engine rpm at 60 mph went up only to 3084 rpm. The Wing's fuel injection provided magnificent throttle response, especially when recalibrated for 1986 on the Aspencade SE-i, but the high cost of fuel injection forced Honda to return to carburetors throughout the GL line for 1987.

But, by then, the Gold Wing's venerable horizontally opposed four-cylinder engine was living on borrowed time. As an engine is made bigger to raise its torque, and spun slower to reduce noise and vibration, its firing impulses become bigger and spaced further apart. This is felt as driveline harshness—the feeling of being propelled by a series of separate impulses or bangs, not by a smooth flow of power. Even the GL's torsional shock absorbers in the driveline couldn't keep the engine from twisting slightly in its mounts as each cylinder fired, delivering its message of fewer, bigger bangs to the rider. There was no escape except to smooth the engine's power flow by increasing the number of cylinders, and consequently the number of power pulses per revolution.

To get the torque required for passing at vibration-suppressing lower rpm, the engine would have to be made bigger as well. With a displacement of 1520cc instead of the previous 1182, the six-cylinder could also be regeared to turn more slowly, yet still deliver increased passing punch. Overall gearing in fifth would be the tallest of any GL, yielding the lowest rpm at 60 mph, 2607 rpm. Another advantage of the six's smoother power delivery was that the heavy flywheel formerly used on the four-cylinder engine to smooth out power pulses was unnecessary. This helped boost acceleration on the six, and gave noticeably snappier throttle response.

A large engine, turning at low cruising rpm, was just the beginning of an overall process of noise and vibration suppression for the Gold Wing. Osamu Sato, the Noise, Vibration and Harshness (NVH) engineer on the GL1500, surveyed the entire motorcycle as though it were an unseen orchestra of subtle musicians. Using microphones and waveform recording and analysis equipment, Sato isolated the players one by one. An unsupported crankcase panel might vibrate at its own natural frequency to make one detectable trace on the oscilloscope screen. A subtle sawtooth wave might come from gear teeth engaging under power. A barely detectable low-frequency signal might come from the crank's motions in its bearings. The job was to isolate, understand and quiet each of these sound sources. This is a process that is not done once and forgotten. It continues to seek and suppress noise as part of the ongoing refinement of design and production. In the case of the 1500, added ribbing stilled the vibrating crankcase panel. For fifth gear, a quieter-running helical pair was substituted for the original straight-cut gears. By putting more tooth pairs in simultaneous contact, helical gears hand off the load from one tooth pair to the next more gradual-

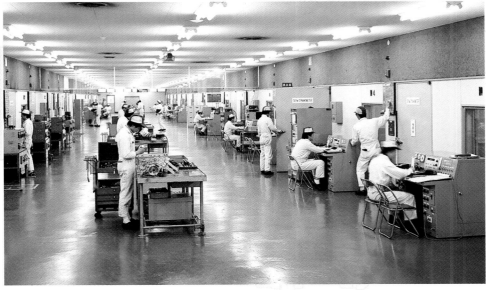

THIS IS WHERE THE MAGIC STARTS—AT *Honda R&D in Japan. Here, rows of dynamometers test engines to the limit during early development.*

ly, reducing noise. Extremely close crank-to-bearing tolerances hold the journals to tighter, quieter orbits.

Tracing the history of the Gold Wing's powertrain reveals another trend, one started by the original GL1000, that has influenced all subsequent motorcycle design: the blending of automotive design elements. One of those elements was automotive-style liquid cooling, attractive for more than one reason. Not only does liquid cooling maintain more consistent engine temperature regardless of power output, it's also much quieter than air cooling, with none of the resonating, sound-radiating qualities associated with air cooling's multitude of fins.

Consistent coolant temperature brings an engine closer to constant clearances between moving parts, thus controlling the noise created by bearings knocking, pistons slapping in their bores and valve tappets clicking. With liquid

THE GL1200'S 1182cc ENGINE PROPELLED A *great leap forward in Gold Wing performance, thanks to increased displacement and standard hot-rod tuning tactics. Tall gearing, though, brought with it an equally big leap in smoothness at cruising rpm.*

STUDY IN SMOOTHNESS: *The GL1500 represents the fourth generation of Gold Wing powerplants, and its shaft drive is the third such iteration. Each one saw concomitant increases in power and smoothness.*

TO GOLD WING OWNERS, SILENCE IS GOLDEN. *Here, Honda employs an anechoic chamber to check GL1500 sound levels.*

HONDA IS CONSTANTLY RESEARCHING NEW *ways to cut gear teeth so that they will transmit their power as silently as possible. Teeth that are helical cut, or split, as in this example, further reduce noise.*

TIMING CHAINS CAN BE NOISY, AS THEY *vibrate along their lengths and slap their rollers against the cam drives. Toothed-rubber belts, such as this one for the Gold Wing, are much quieter.*

cooling, all of these noise-producing clearances can be set and held much tighter. Honda went even further, though, adopting open-deck construction, in which the tops of the cylinders are not connected to the water jackets at all. Now there is no solid metal path for piston-generated sound—it has to pass through the coolant. Quiet.

Another related bit of automotive technology is the current GL1500's liquid-heated manifold. Such a piece was part of the original M1, and returned on the six-cylinder as part of a comprehensive program to tightly control carburetion both for ridability and emissions reasons. By heating the intake manifold with coolant and using the exhaust manifold to heat intake air during warm-up, the fuel from the carbs is forced to evaporate and form an easily ignited vapor that reduces hesitation.

Yet another bit of auto technology is the GL's shaft drive. The Gold Wing was Honda's first production motorcycle driven by shaft, and as such pioneered uncharted engineering ground. To speed the M1 prototype process, Honda borrowed the back end of a BMW, but a production machine needed its own design, one

that turned into a torturous, near-two-year odyssey for Hirotake Takahashi, charged with developing a final drive for the GL1000.

The gear pair connecting the drive shaft and rear wheel were central to the whole design. First, these gears had to be bulletproof. Drag-strip starts, missed shifts, and pothole impacts subject these gears to great loads because the rear tire, being so much larger than the gear, has powerful leverage over it. Successful gears would have to tolerate intense abuse. The gears would also have to be as silent as possible. The process by which one tooth pair passes its load to the next pair must not excite vibration or noise, which meant the tooth forms would have to be highly accurate.

Ordinary gears, such as those in hoists or electric tools, can be designed straight out of standard handbooks; heavily loaded power gearing is another matter, as Takahashi would discover. The engineers devised an *ad-hoc* gear torture which they called the hop test, to simulate the worst of what might happen to gears in actual use. A test rider would ride at about 30 mph, shift to neutral, then stomp the transmission into first. Thereupon the rear wheel would hop violently against the pavement, repeating the impact as many as 20 times, exerting up to two tons of thrust force on the gear teeth and three-and-a-half tons of lateral thrust. This crude test was Takahashi's nemesis, cracking gearcases like eggs. Endless combinations of material, tooth pitch and form, heat-treating and surface-hardening methods and depth were tried. All of them broke.

Takahashi finally came to believe the gears themselves might not be the problem. If the gearcase was flexing, it might concentrate load at the fragile edges of the teeth, causing early failure. He tested this idea by observing the movement of the tooth-to-tooth contact

pattern as torque was applied in a test rig; it moved from the middle of the teeth toward the edge. Improved case designs followed, with more testing. Once the gears were supported rigidly enough to control the movement of the contact zone, gearcases and gears survived the torture tests, and engineers were on their way to producing Honda's first motorcycle shaft drive.

Much like the engine, the Gold Wing's chassis underwent near constant revision and development. Customer voices grew more specific, and Honda gained confidence both in them and the GL's increasingly well-defined mission as a long-distance touring bike. A chassis offers a dizzying array of interconnected variables, with seemingly small changes affecting other areas. While altering a car's interior for greater comfort has little effect on handling, the same cannot be said for a motorcycle. Customer insistence on more room and greater luxury led inevitably to greater weight and longer wheelbases. Concern for a low seat height led to shorter rear-wheel travel and its corresponding effect on ride quality.

With more weight and a longer wheelbase, the search for steering ease prompted endless combinations of tire and wheel sizes, tire construction and frame geometry changes. Chassis development proceeded slowly at first in the GL1000 family, with changes limited almost entirely to the 1978 model. Customers wished for greater suspension compliance. To that end, Honda chamfered the lower ends of the fork stanchion tubes as a means of enticing oil into the clearances between the fork tube bushings and the slider. Fork travel also went up an inch, and the bike benefited from a new, plusher saddle.

A more productive period of chassis development came with the GL1100 family. Starting with the first model in 1980, Honda engineers again attempted to deal with fork stiction, this time fitting each fork leg with two of the new Syntallic™ lead/Teflon® friction-reducing slider bushings, and increasing fork tube diameter by 2mm to 39mm for greater rigidity.

Both front and rear suspension systems also supported most of their load with air pressure, with steel springs playing a minor role. Air as a suspension medium had come into vogue through motocross racing in the 1970s and then in road racing. For touring applications, it offered desirable advantages in seat height and load capacity. Touring riders wanted a low seat, but a low saddle rules out long-travel suspension

for soaking up bumps. One way to achieve compliance with limited wheel-travel is to make the spring rate progressive—soft at first for ride comfort, but progressively stiffer to prevent bottoming. Those are precisely the characteristics of air, and Honda used this advantage to help lower the 1980 GL1100's saddle 0.6 inch compared to the '79's. Air also allows quick, easy ride-height adjustment to accommodate the variations in loads a touring bike must deal with.

The need for greater comfort also led to a dramatic, 2.4-inch growth in wheelbase in 1980. Half of this additional length came from the frame itself, and half from a longer swingarm. Honda also increased rake from 28 degrees to 29.2, and lengthened trail from 4.7 inches to 5.3 inches to balance the steering response with straight-line handling. The 1982 model pushed rake out even further, bumping it to 29.8 degrees, and pulling trail back fractionally to 5.2 inches. The geometry changes were partly a result of fresh rolling stock: 1-inch-smaller-diameter wheels (18-inch in front, 16-inch in back), with wider rims and bigger tires (120/90 vs. 110/90 in front, 140/90 vs. 130/90 at the rear). That move alone boosted gross vehicle load capacity by 25 pounds. An on-board air compressor for the Aspencade model allowed quick, easy alteration of rear ride height. Rear suspension travel also got chopped 1.2 inches, down to 3.1 inches, the shortest travel of the entire GL family.

Suspension continued to be the main thrust of GL development for the 1983 model. By now, Honda's racing experience provided lessons that allowed the use of more sophisticated dampers and springs to accomplish what had been done previously with air assist. As a result, fork compression damping increased, as did spring rates—the rear springs were stiffened a whopping 50 percent—allowing less

CRANKCASE WEBBING MAKES THE CASES stronger and more rigid—and much less able to vibrate and generate noise. This and other strengthening techniques are key to the Gold Wing's quiet running.

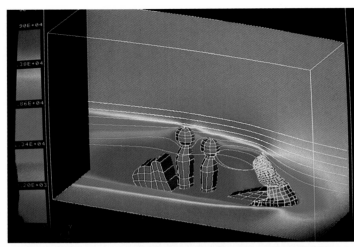

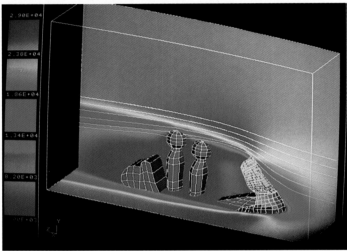

LIKE ANY MODERN MANUFACTURER, HONDA makes extensive use of Computer Aided Design (CAD), such as in this wind tunnel simulation. Computer assisted design saves time and money at every step, reducing the number of mock-ups and prototypes that must be built, and shortening time from the drawing board to the production line.

reliance on air pressure. Air would remain as a spring-assist medium on this and successive Gold Wings, but it would never again carry as much of the bike's weight as it originally had.

Honda also fitted a TRAC (Torque Reactive Anti-dive Control) system to the '83-model fork. As the rider applied the brakes, a hinged front caliper would restrict compression damping circuits in the fork, increasing compression damping and reducing front-end dive. Other changes included making more room for the passenger via a 1.2-inch-longer seat, and by moving the trunk back and up.

The following year saw the GL's second major redesign, with the phenomenal GL1200. The GL1200 set new standards of comfort, ride and handling, and no part of the chassis went untouched. A new frame with the steering head moved down and back brought the engine forward 2.5 inches for more legroom, and put more weight on the front end. A 2.2-inch-longer swing arm also shifted weight forward, and helped contribute to a slightly longer wheelbase. Steering geometry balanced slightly greater rake—30 degrees vs. 29.2—with a significant drop in trail—4.6 inches vs. 5.2. Bigger, 41mm fork tubes provided a more rigid path for steering inputs.

Honda also turned to smaller-diameter wheels and tires to decrease steering effort on the 1200. Wheel size went down to then-fashionable 16-inch in front, with a 15-incher at the rear. Tire sizes grew to 130/90 in front and 150/90 in back, putting more rubber on the road. The suspension itself, having to deal with ever increasing weight, was completely recalibrated. Wheel travel increased to 5.5 inches in front and 4.1 inches in back (5.3 and 3.1 inches previously), yet the new frame helped keep seat height down to 30.7 inches—0.4 inch lower than before. To help damp chassis

motion over the increased travel, Honda stiffened the suspension, and fitted two TRAC units—one for each fork leg. The dual TRAC allowed Honda to reduce compression damping by 20 percent in the fork, increasing bump compliance. With these changes to the chassis, the 1984 GL1200 set unapproachably high standards for steering response and ride quality.

These significant chassis changes carried the 1200 through its remaining years. Further chassis development would wait for the GL1500 six-cylinder's debut in 1988. And, just as the 1100 and 1200 before it, the 1500 would benefit from the entire body of knowledge Honda had acquired in the interim.

The 1500 would provide fresh opportunities to solve old problems, too. Once again, a new frame saw wheelbase grow to its longest yet—66.9 inches—for more room. Weight increased to almost 800 pounds, and Honda selected wider and larger-diameter rolling stock, with wheel sizes up to 18 inches in front and 16 inches in back. As you can see, this is looking like a formula for extraordinarily slow, heavy steering. Yet the GL1500, like its predecessor, again set new standards for its class in handling. How?

Through racing, Honda had discovered that frame rigidity had a profound effect on handling response. On light, racing chassis, fork, frame and swing arm can flex as road forces bend and twist them, degrading handling response. Make the components stiffer and handling ease can be regained through less conservative steering geometry and careful tire selection.

Before this knowledge could be incorporated in the GL1500, however, another controversy had to be resolved. The chassis engineers wanted to achieve the maximum frame stiffness by bolting the engine solidly as a stressed member—a practice used in all previous Gold Wings. But the engine designers, knowing that even a flat-six has higher-order vibrations that can be annoying, insisted upon rubber mounting. Test motorcycles had to be constructed and evaluated, and the final decision was to go with rubber mounting. That, in turn, put the burden of achieving higher stiffness onto the chassis department.

To achieve the desired chassis strength and balance, engineers utilized Computer Aided Design (CAD) to find the center of gravity for different chassis configurations. To predict control forces and speed of response, the polar moments of the machine were measured on special balances. These methods acted as a kind of filter, eliminating obviously unpromising chassis configurations, and the extra time it would have taken to build and test such prototypes. Honda's involvement with racing also provided additional direction in chassis design. The GL1500's frame consists of a pair of massive main beams that go directly from steering head to swing-arm pivot, just as they do on Honda's 200-mph NSR500 Grand Prix bikes. The ultra-rigid and carefully balanced chassis contributed to steering response that was even lighter than previous Gold Wings' despite a much longer wheelbase and greater total weight.

Tires play another key role in handling. Generally, wide, round-profile tires with large contact patches tend to give higher steering effort than narrower, more triangular ones. Tire design is not as simple as the difference between narrow and wide, rounded and triangular, though. The invisible angles and stiffness of the cord plies in a tire have similar effects. Plies with their fibers running more parallel to the tire's rotational direction give greater stiffness and faster steering response, while plies angled across the carcass from bead to bead tend to produce a more flexible and slower-steering tire. Bias-belted construction—originally developed for racing applications—combines characteristics of both, giving a soft sidewall for a compliant ride, yet still offering a stiff tread region for a low wear rate and sharp steering response. Diligent testing with an almost endless series of prototypes from Dunlop produced bias-belted tires for the GL1500 that give the bike much of its remarkably responsive handling.

Racing also assisted with the GL1500's suspension. Honda engineers instrumented the suspension on motocross machines, and discovered that damper valves open and close at rates far higher than previously believed. They found similarly high damper valve speeds in road racing, and realized these rapid closure rates made conventional dampers essentially rigid at such high speeds. When the GL1500's

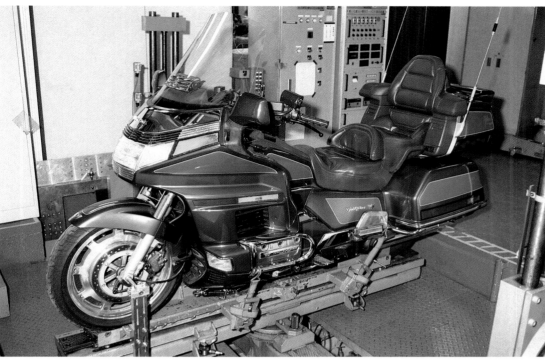

damper valving was designed to take account of this, ride quality over rough surfaces reached new levels of compliance. This highly developed technology has also allowed the suspension to take back some of the suspension function that had been handed to fatter tires over the years, further contributing to longer tire life.

Motorcycle touring will never come to an end, and therefore there will never be an ultimate Gold Wing. As long as touring riders continue to seek perfection, the established partnership between Honda and Gold Wing riders will continue to yield fresh designs. This and the constant flow of advanced technology from a variety of sources within Honda's R&D centers guarantee that more capable, luxurious and comfortable Gold Wings await us in the years ahead.

THIS COMPUTERIZED TEST JIG MEASURES center of mass, long a key element to the Gold Wing's light steering and balanced chassis. Systems such as this—that measure polar moment of inertia and gather other data crucial to the way a motorcycle steers and responds to rider inputs—helped Honda pioneer mass centralization in the early days of development, and have heavily influenced the way Honda designs and builds motorcycles, from exotic Grand Prix racing machines to production street bikes. The Gold Wing, with its fuel tank located underneath the seat, played a key role in mass centralization technology from the very beginning.

ENDLESS TESTING AND THE conflicting demands of rigidity, weight and cost drove development of the GL1500's frame for one-and-a-half years. Insistance upon rubber engine mounts precluded using the engine as a stressed member and made the solution more difficult. The end result was 1.5 times stiffer than its predecessor.

MOTORCYCLES DON'T SPRING INTO LIFE FULLY realized, as if from the head of Zeus. The path to market, whether it's a brand-new design or a complete makeover, stretches far longer. Concepts must be born, sketches drawn and approved. The process can be driven by market research, or begin simply as a designer's dream. Often, designs are tested with a series of focus groups around the country, or even around the world.

In the case of the Gold Wing, it is easy to understand the importance of research. Over the years, Gold Wing design has trod a fine line between progress and familiarity. The GL1500 styling in particular had to look familiar enough to attract traditionalists, but also progressive enough to remain contemporary years after its introduction.

At Honda, almost anyone can come up with a concept for a new or updated motorcycle, the sort of idea usually preceded by the thought, "Wouldn't it be neat if we ...?" From there, design teams begin a series of sketches, and if they generate sufficient enthusiasm the project can take on a momentum of its own, perhaps carrying all the way to the production line.

In the more formalized design process, the first step includes research and brainstorming sessions to outline the bike's concept. This is pure blue-sky stuff; at this stage the designers have almost unlimited freedom, and their imaginations can run pretty wild. Here's where you'll see such things as electro/hydraulic mainstands, or hidden exhaust systems, or any other sort of outlandish ideas fertile minds can conjure up. Such ideas might come from the designers themselves, or anywhere within the company, and they sometimes influence engineering.

Depending on the project, the number of sketches at this blue-sky stage can range from dozens up to about 100. Then meetings are held to evaluate the sketches, and include people from the concept, sales, marketing, and engineering staffs. At this point, engineers offer their input on what, conceptually, can or can't be done, with suggestions on what direction the bike should take.

The engineers then develop a layout sketch based on the meeting's outcome that determines basic specifications, including engine location, seat height, wheelbase, steering geometry and so on. Designers then work up another series of renderings, called tight sketches, using the dimensions from the layout sketches. Some 10 to 30 of these tight sketches might be generated, and they're subject to further review. Once a single sketch is

Here, designers and modelers work to create a three-dimensional representation of the bike in clay. Again, depending on the project, the clay base—the chassis—might be a custom, one-off piece, or simply assembled from existing parts. An armature, made of wood or plastic, is applied to the clay base to support the heavy clay, and designers and modelers begin to sculpt the clay to match the approved sketch. Much interpretation is possible at this stage, perhaps because the sketch offers a limited num- ber of views, or perhaps because the design lends itself to different interpretations. In the case of two competing designs, modelers might even sculpt one on each side of the same bike in the clay.

During this phase, engineers offer their input almost daily, guided by the realities of production. Many of the small parts—instruments, footpeg brackets, mufflers and so on—will go through several generations as they're drawn and fabricated. Finally, the clay mock-up will be modeled to a near-finished look, and then subject to a design review that measures the model against the engineering department's layout drawings.

Before final approval, yet another clay mock-up is made, from which to generate plastic body parts for a final mock-up, or later for a running prototype (mock-ups are always non-running models of the design). The FRP (fiberglass-reinforced-plastic) parts might be molded straight off the clay, or the clay might be precisely measured, with the numbers fed into a numerically controlled milling machine, which then creates plaster molds for the plastic parts.

Once approved, a final clay mock-up is made, sculpted precisely to engineering specifications. At this point, the design's symmetry is complete; if there were two competing designs, one will have been discarded. Then designers add color, laying water-soaked sheets of flexible vinyl over the clay—much like applying a decal—or

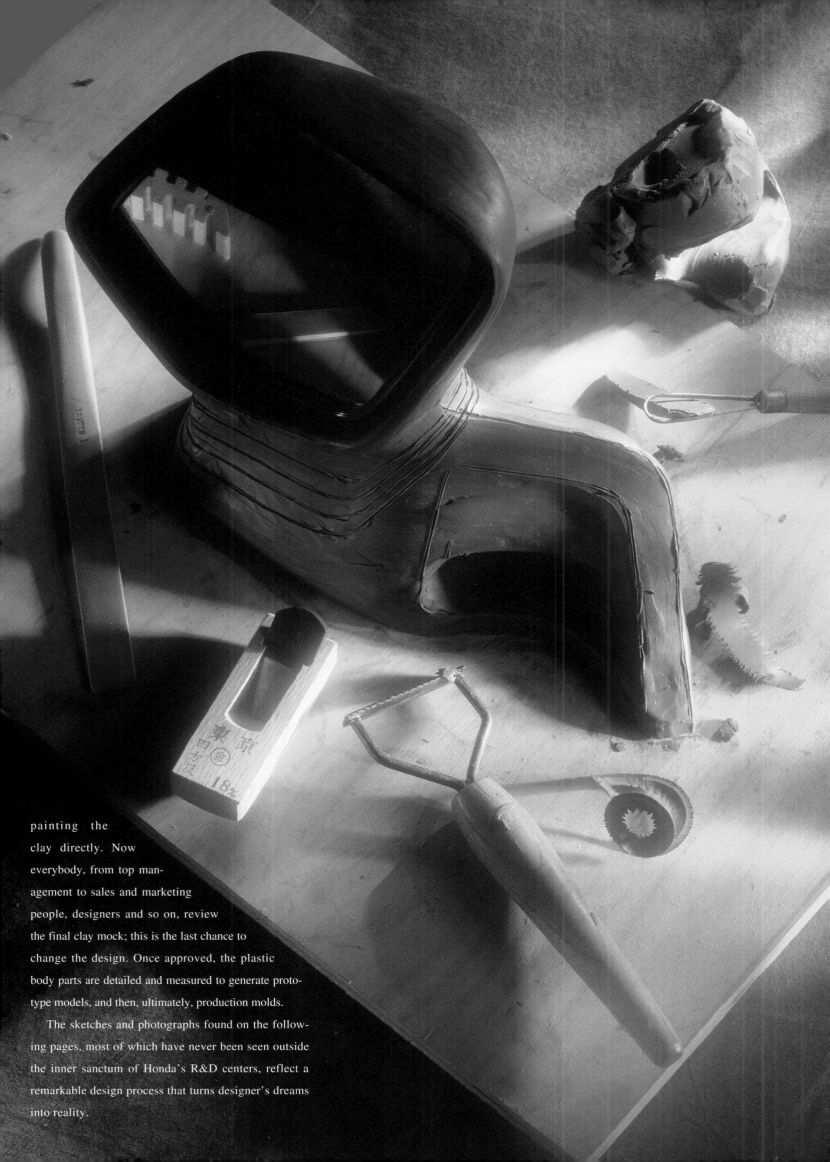

painting the clay directly. Now everybody, from top management to sales and marketing people, designers and so on, review the final clay mock; this is the last chance to change the design. Once approved, the plastic body parts are detailed and measured to generate prototype models, and then, ultimately, production molds.

The sketches and photographs found on the following pages, most of which have never been seen outside the inner sanctum of Honda's R&D centers, reflect a remarkable design process that turns designer's dreams into reality.

A prototype for the first GL1000 Gold Wing. In Honda parlance, prototypes are running motorcycles; mock-ups are non-runners for design study. This one is an actual test bike for early Gold Wing development.

An early GL mock-up, with instrument pod on the dummy tank as on the production models in 1978 and 1979. This is a full mock-up in metal, and as such shows its age. At the time, Honda made mock-ups in plastic, fiberglass or metal, lacking the technique for clay modeling the firm currently uses. Note the four mufflers, inspired by the CB750.

This second-generation GL1000 Gold Wing mock-up was used to explore different color and styling ideas. Soichiro Honda himself dictated the styling on this one. He didn't like the flattop, teardrop-shape dummy fuel tanks of earlier mock-ups, and wanted instead a more rounded, humpback fuel-tank shape reminiscent of Honda Grand Prix road race bikes of the '60s and early '70s. The teardrop shape won for production, though.

This late-stage, first-generation mock-up for the GL1000 still sports GX750 badges. Mr. Honda was at first reluctant to enter the big-displacement category, so engineers kept the 750 badges on the mock-up until testing data quantified the decision to go with a bigger engine.

One of the original design-concept sketches for the standard-version GL1200, rendered in April 1982, with a gas tank similar to that of Honda's Sabre models. Designers have the most freedom at this stage in the styling process.

Another first-generation mock-up, still with GX750 badges, shows Honda was experimenting with fairings in 1973, long before the Interstate model in 1980. Notice the differences between this and the other GX750-badged mock-up, including the fork, brake caliper location, and the cylinder head.

With this GL1200 Aspencade concept sketch, the designer stepped into uncharted territory, with passenger floorboards that eventually made it into production, and a fairing design and folding passenger-armrests that did not. The front wheel looks similar to that of the later-model GL1500, albeit with a vented internal front brake system similar to that found years later on the VT250.

Closer yet. The fairing looks much more like the production GL1200 version, and so does the exhaust system, but the armrests continue to hang on, as does the inboard front brake system. This is a Honda Japan design sketch, rendered in response to HRA sketches.

Getting closer, but still experimenting. This concept sketch of the GL1200 came from Honda Research of America (HRA) in March 1982. The folding armrests and passenger floorboards remain, but now the exhaust has the bologna-slice outlet seen a year later on Honda's Nighthawks.

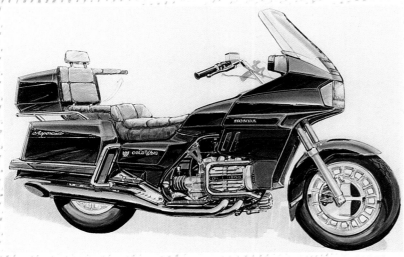

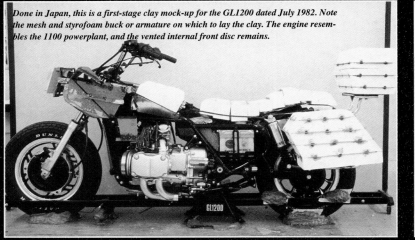

Done in Japan, this is a first-stage clay mock-up for the GL1200 dated July 1982. Note the mesh and styrofoam buck or armature on which to lay the clay. The engine resembles the 1100 powerplant, and the vented internal front disc remains.

As the modelers and designers continue to shape the clay, notice how the surfaces—including the saddle—gain definition. Also, note how the saddlebags and trunk change size and shape as the design is modified through different stages.

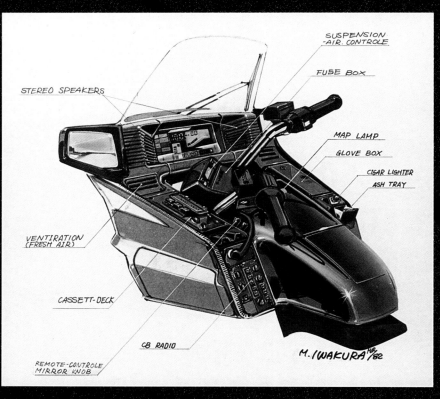

SUSPENSION -AIR. CONTROLE

FUSE BOX

STEREO SPEAKERS

MAP LAMP

GLOVE BOX

CIGAR LIGHTER

ASH TRAY

VENTIRATION (FRESH AIR)

CASSETT-DECK

CB RADIO

M. IWAKURA '82

REMOTE-CONTROLE MIRROR KNOB

This 1982 HRA sketch illustrates just how many of the designer's ideas made it into production. Those familiar with the GL1200 will recognize the digital display for the instruments, storage area in the fairing pocket, speaker location and vent registers. But the map light, cigar lighter, ashtray and remote-control mirrors didn't make it past the stylist's rendering. Nor did the windshield wiper, which scratched the Lexan windshield in testing.

This is a styling proposal mock-up for the 1985 GL1200 Gold Wing Interstate. Close to the final version, it lacks the production model's trunk.

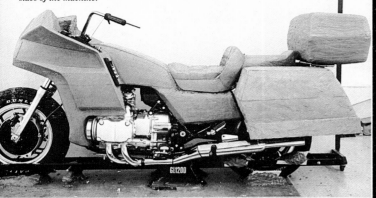

Further definition comes in the seat, saddlebag and fairing areas, as designers begin to prepare the surface for finishing, and match contours on both sides of the machine.

A later-generation clay mock-up, adding still more detail, includes badges, reflectors, handlebar controls, radio and CB antennae, passenger floorboards, and engine and saddlebag guards.

Honda's clay modelers are true artisans, as evidenced by the detail found in the finished clay mock-up. Remarkably lifelike in every detail, the bike is somewhat heavy, and the saddle probably wouldn't do for an all-day ride. ...

Model makers are artists of the highest skill. In their hands, lumps of clay become startlingly realistic mock-ups, as they bring three-dimensional life to designers' drawings.

A similar mock-up, with paint and graphics applied, looks good enough to be ridden away. Such accuracy leaves nothing to interpretation in the final design review.

This plastic mock-up of the GL1200 might have been molded directly off an earlier clay mock-up, or from plaster molds milled on numerically controlled machines with measurements taken from a clay mock...

Another styling exercise for the GL1200, but with the cowling added for 1987. The front wheel design looks remarkably like that seen the following year on the GL1500 Gold Wing.

An early concept sketch from December 1983 for the GL1500. At this point, Honda was still divided about the engine's ultimate configuration and displacement; the rendering identifies this as a GL1300. Note the heads-up display with time and road speed on the windshield.

At the time of this concept sketch—dated February 1984—the engine was a fuel-injected 1400 four-cylinder, although the rendering still identifies it as a 1300. The rider's portion of the saddle now has an adjustable backrest, and you can see the first design indication of the GL1500's distinctive front end treatment.

Dated May 1984, this sketch of a blue Aspencade shows the fairing and front wheel treatment progressing toward production, but the engine's back to 1300cc, with no fuel-injection badges.

Another May 1984 sketch, this one features a saddle of small proportions, big wheels
and tires, a push-button control panel for the passenger, and a 1400cc engine still in
the traditional GL horizontally opposed four-cylinder architecture.

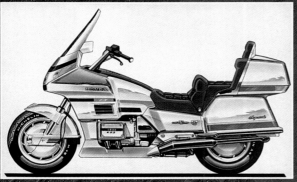

By June of 1984, this white Aspencade is
beginning to sport some unusual features.
Note, for example, the single spring/shock
unit under the bike, working in tension
rather than compression, plus the push-
buttons on the saddle for pneumatic
adjustment of the seat cushion and lumbar
support. Also, a running light has been
added to the front brake cowling.

This sketch from July 1984 shows how close the bodywork—especially the
saddlebags and trunk—are coming to final production. You can see another version of the single-shock suspension under the bike, as well as the front wheel running light. The engine has again become a fuel-injected, 1400cc flat-four.

Penned in October 1984, this sketch shows the Gold
Wing pushing toward a more sport-touring role. The
engine's displacement—as well as its configuration—
is still under discussion. Notice how the designer tries
to influence engineering, with an electro/hydraulic-
operated mainstand and hidden exhaust system. Note
also the rounded treatment of the saddlebags, similar
to what would appear on Honda's Pacific Coast.

On this full-size, three-dimensional mock-up, various details inch closer to production. By now, the bodywork is almost finalized, but the engine has grown to 1500cc—although still a flat-four—and still features a hidden exhaust. The seat has yet another version of the pivoting backrest.

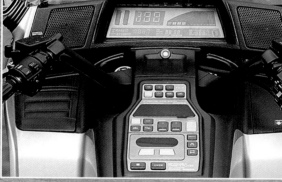

Rider's-eye view shows the remarkable detail Honda modelers achieve even with a mock-up. Note the detachable cassette deck, trip computer, and digital display for the instrument panel.

Another full-size three-dimensional mock-up, this one dates from April of 1985. Honda often does parallel development of competing designs, in this case producing two similar mock-ups for both four-cylinder and six-cylinder engine concepts. The bodywork on this mock-up is plastic, the engine is wood.

By August of 1985, GL1500 designers had approval to build a clay mock-up with a six-cylinder engine. Notice the separate carbs and exhaust headers for each cylinder.

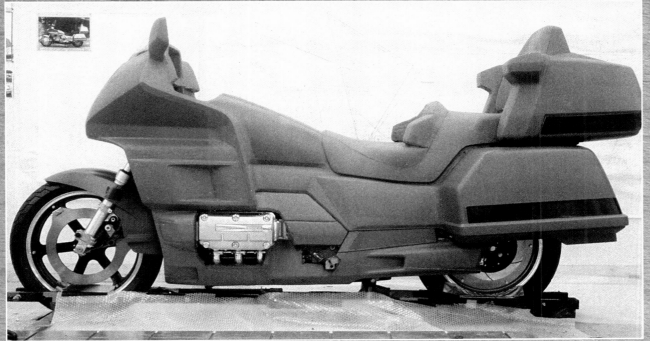

A month later, the clay begins to take rough shape. It looks as though the hidden muffler system still has appeal to the designers. Also note the brake system; both front and rear brake rotors bolt to the wheel rim areas, with inverted calipers that grip the rotors' inner surfaces.

A final full-size mock-up of the 1500 Gold Wing, just prior to production. The wooden engine reflects what the production powerplant would become. Many of the details, such as the rear wheel configuration and hidden exhaust, will be altered for production.

Here are two different mock-ups of the instrument panel and controls. You can see how the elaborate bar-mounted push-button controls, digital instruments and detachable cassette and clock were either simplified or abandoned for the production version. Notice in the digital version, though, the warning light for a parking brake: Honda originally considered an automatic transmission for the GL1500.

To Helsinki And Back

70,000 MILES AND 43 COUNTRIES IN
752 DAYS—ON A GOLD WING.

JARI SAARELAINEN LAY SLEEPING ON THE deck of a river boat, floating lazily across the River Siak in Indonesia. Weaving deep into the heart of the Asian jungles, this river is a lifeline for the villagers and crocodiles who share its murky water. On this dark night, Saarelainen, who'd left his native Finland 18 months earlier on a world tour, had just settled in next to his GL1500 when a sudden, violent crash shocked him back into consciousness. He awoke to see the massive bow of an oil tanker towering above him.

The tanker tore into the little river boat, tossing it aside. Jari struggled to salvage valuables from his Gold Wing—passport, money, anything—but it all happened too fast. He had just enough time to grab a flashlight before the boat and his Gold Wing sank beneath him. The ship went down in less than two minutes.

In the darkness, the current carried him and other passengers down river. One of the group had already vanished and would never be found. Jari hung onto floating debris, until a local fisherman who had heard

NOT EXACTLY TYPICAL GL TER-
ritory. But, then, Jari Saarelainen's
around-the-world adventure wasn't
your typical tour. Not surprisingly, he
fried his clutch in the Sahara sands.

DANGLING LIKE THE CATCH OF THE DAY,
Jari's GL gets fished from the drink in the River Siak
in Indonesia.

WITH THE NEAREST HONDA DEALER LITERAL-
ly thousands of miles away, Jari often had to rely on
the kindness of strangers for help.

the collision plucked him out of the river more than a mile downstream. "We probably would have ended up as crocodile bait," said Jari.

Hours later, when the sun finally rose, Jari made his way back to civilization to organize the rescue of his Gold Wing, money, passport, clothes and everything else that lay at the bottom of the river. Jari's Gold Wing and valuables were retrieved—while well-armed soldiers stood guard over the divers, watching for crocodiles—and the bike was repaired in Singapore and emerged looking and running like new. He was lucky. The River Siak incident not only nearly ended his trip—it almost ended his life.

That was only one of many sidebars to the story of Jari Saarelainen's around-the-world adventure. He lost the clutch in axle-deep sand in the Sahara, and had to drive 1500 miles one-way to get new parts. He slid down into an icy, snow-covered Andean valley, only to have traction disappear completely on the way out the other side. He was stuck in the African outback with a flat, and the only shop around for several hundred miles charged him $600 for a Taiwanese front tire. In El Salvador, he was close enough to hear the machine guns crackle as the guerrillas clashed with the army, and he sat on the road for hours waiting for the battle to move on and traffic lanes to reopen. It's hard to imagine these things all happening to one person, let alone all on one trip. Yet all this and more confronted Jari during his 752-day-long trip around the world.

In what the Guinness Book of Records certified as the longest solo motorcycle trip around the world, the 30-year-old Finnish Gold Wing rider left Helsinki on January 12, 1989, and for the next two years rode his bike south across Europe and Africa, then turned right, crossing South, Central and North America, Australia, then Asia before heading back to Europe again. Along the way he burned almost 2300 gallons of gasoline and racked up close to 70,000 miles in 43 countries—on a Gold Wing GL1500 that already had more than 50,000 miles on the odometer

before the trip began. During his journey, Jari covered every kind of terrain you can possibly traverse on a Gold Wing, including some you probably shouldn't.

Jari had originally planned to travel with a partner, who understandably bowed out when faced with a two-year hiatus from normal life. Undaunted, Jari took off on his own, traveling the first few thousand miles through Europe with his sister piloting another bike. Once he reached Africa, however, he was on his own.

That doesn't mean that he was alone, though, because during his passage Jari met a broad cross-section of humanity, including fellow motorcyclists, transplanted Finns, general well-wishers and otherwise envious travelers, as well as the occasional ne'er-do-well. Included in this last group was the bar-hopping banker in Brazil. Offering a 25-percent improvement over the official exchange rate, this glib con man changed a lump of cash for a lick and a promise, leaving Jari in a dark alley in Rio de Janeiro, $100 poorer but considerably wiser for the experience.

But by far the trip reaffirmed Jari's faith in his fellow man. Rarely did he reach a major city without offers of free food or lodging. His bike received equally hospitable treatment, spending nights everywhere from hotel rooms to the nave of a church. More often than not, the rare mishap—mechanical or otherwise—was met with sympathetic ears and helping hands.

Early on, one fellow traveler gave him an invaluable bit of advice fit for any worldwide tourist: Money talks. Throughout his trip, the Honda rider carried a generous supply of "speaking dollars." In some underdeveloped countries, the effect of a U.S. $10 bill on reluctant bureaucrats—especially customs officials—was sometimes nothing short of astonishing.

Jari's story caught people's interest everywhere. The sight of an abused, unwashed Gold Wing in the wilds of Central Africa or the Amazonian jungle is sure to draw some attention. Even in more civilized locales, the overburdened bike with the Finnish plates aroused people's curiosity. The six-cylinder Honda gave him instant access to anyone who had owned, ridden or wished for a motorcycle. It made him an instant celebrity in some of the most unlikely locales, including the Himalayas, where the bike got him a meeting with the King of Bhutan, who was also a motorcyclist.

Like an ice-cream truck at an elementary school, the GL drew onlookers by the dozens. It was a particular hit with the local members of law enforcement—too

much so, on several occasions, such as the time Jari nearly ran over a traffic cop who raised his hand and stepped directly in front of the bike in Mexico City. After wrestling the bike to a full-panic halt, he found the officer simply wanted a closer look at this exotic machine, and a chance to chat with the fellow from such a distant country.

Equally astonishing was the number of times the crowd included a transplanted Finn, an acquaintance or—on numerous occasions—an old friend. Finland might seem a small country to most travelers, but Jari's luck at finding people from his past underscored the cliché about this small world we live in.

During his tour, he appeared in countless newspaper features and faced numerous TV interviews—including one humorous incident in which a non-English-speaking video editor mixed up the interviewer's questions and Jari's responses: Q: "So, how do you like Brazil?" A: "Oh, the Sahara is beautiful, but very dangerous."

Dangerous, indeed. During his trek through the Sahara, Jari had another brush with disaster. The Sahara claims dozens of lives every year, and crossing it on a heavy motorcycle invites disaster. The deep sand swallowed the Gold Wing's wheels constantly, forcing him to dig out every few miles. After two days of climbing out of sand pits, the GL's clutch finally burned out, leaving him stranded. Luckily, he was on a well-trav-

eled road and was able to hitch a ride with a German couple in a van. After a slow, four-day ride he arrived in Guezzam, then moved on to Niger where he was able to order parts from Finland. The parts arrived in Niamey, the capital city of Niger. With no shipping routes, he had to travel to the capital himself to get the parts, and travel back to make the repairs—a grueling, 3000-mile, three-week round trip.

Those of us who've never reached past our own borders can take a lesson from Jari Saarelainen's adventure. Time and again, his travels took him into situations where he had to trust in the kindness of strangers, and rarely was that trust misplaced. In some cases their help was a mere courtesy, in others it was potentially life-saving. Whether it was a much-needed lift through the sands of the Sahara in a battered Mercedes van, or a complete bike overhaul at American Honda in Torrance, California, Jari found people's generosity almost overwhelming.

It's not merely what he did, or what others did for him, that make the trip so memorable. What he saw—from the sands of the Sahara to the jungles of the Amazon, from the stark grandeur of the Alps to the lush rain forest of the Andes—will last a lifetime. But that, apparently, isn't enough for him. It wasn't long after he arrived home that he began to plan another trip. "And this one," he says, "will be even bigger."

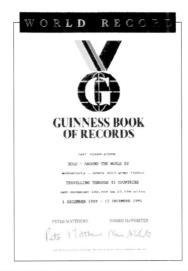

THE PAYOFF: JARI'S CERTIFICATE FROM THE Guinness Book of Records. What did he do with his 15 minutes of fame? Why, he planned another trip, of course. A longer one.

WILD WINGS

GOLD WING RECREATION—WITH NO RULES.

HISTORY DOES NOT RECORD WHAT THE first fledgling Gold Wing alteration was, but chances are it was a functional modification aimed at improving long-term comfort or convenience. Early Wings left the factory undressed, and the addition of aftermarket fairings and saddlebags soon became popular modifications. But as the years passed, and the Gold Wing came right from the factory equipped with many of the touring amenities that cross-country riders yearned for, the modifications moved from the functional to, well, something a bit more expressive.

Today, a substantial number of Wingers see the standard motorcycle as a clean slate, a challenge to their creativity. And a few hardy individuals see possibilities never imagined by Honda engineers in their wildest dreams. Here, we present a selection of some of the wildest Wings you'll ever see.

BONNEVILLE BULLET

Kenny Lyon likes to tour a little differently from most Gold Wing riders. His idea of the perfect cross-country trip is a straight line from one side of the Bonneville Salt Flats to the other. As quickly as possible. The 24-foot-long bullet that's taking shape in his Compton, California, workshop should do better than 232 mph on the Salt— fast enough to break the single-engine streamliner record that's stood since 1972, and to make it the fastest Gold Wing of all time.

A surprisingly stock GL1500 engine will supply the roughly 150 horsepower required to push Lyon's 33-inch high torpedo to a new record. A turbocharger will deliver the extra engine breathing needed, while special cam covers will narrow the engine by 2 inches to reduce wind resistance. Internally, the engine will be largely unmodified.

Lyon has piloted this chassis many times before with smaller powerplants in the engine bay and clocked speeds of up to 217 mph. But with the new-found power of the Honda six-cylinder, he and his streamliner will be venturing to new and uncharted velocities. Lyon is already looking far beyond. With the right salt conditions—and the Gold Wing tweaked to produce 300 horsepower—he figures he could touch 300 mph. Now that's touring!

A TURBOCHARGER SHOULD GIVE Kenny Lyon's GL the wings it needs to go 232 mph on Bonneville's Salt Flats, and perhaps even break the motorcycle land speed record that's stood since 1972.

GOLDEN WING

Wingers just naturally seem to congregate. When they do, motorcycles are compared, stories are swapped, and old friendships rekindled. And a certain amount of good-natured one-upmanship has been known to occur. Hans and Barbara Hagen, an Austrian couple, have a Wing that's difficult to top. And as a happy side effect, the bike has delivered a sharp spike in the economy of the Austrian plating industry.

Hans and Barbara were thrilled with their stock Honda, until they attended a European Gold Wing rally in the summer of '90. Stock would no longer be good enough. After four months of planning, a shipment of 238 pounds of accessories arrived from the United States, and the 1990 GL1500 was completely disassembled. All the chrome bits were shuttled off to be plated with 24 karat gold. Barbara spent over a year hand-engraving the gold-plated parts with unique and elaborate motifs. A Western-inspired (engraved, naturally) saddle was custom made. Other necessities are well attended to: There's a cellular phone, a Monument Valley motif engraved into the windshield, and a custom-built instrument console.

All the elaborate and expensive detail work hasn't turned this Gold Wing into a static display, though. It's often glimpsed rolling along the high-mountain passes of the Alps, where even the mountain goats snatch a second glance.

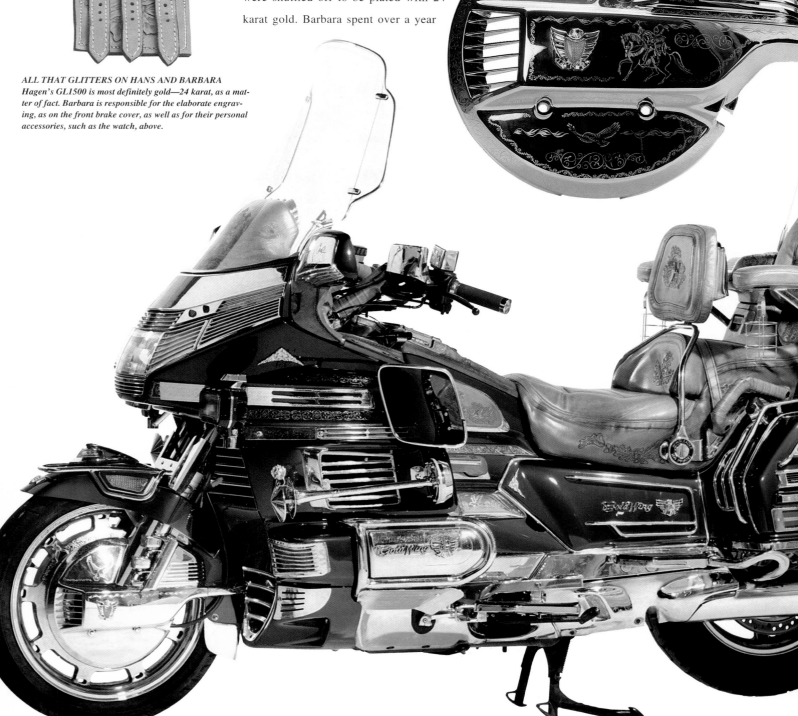

ALL THAT GLITTERS ON HANS AND BARBARA Hagen's GL1500 is most definitely gold—24 karat, as a matter of fact. Barbara is responsible for the elaborate engraving, as on the front brake cover, as well as for their personal accessories, such as the watch, above.

THREE-WHEELERS

With all the amenities that come standard on the Gold Wing, some owners take the next logical step: If two wheels are good, three must be better. A number of companies make trike conversions for the Gold Wing—some so clean they look like they rolled off the Honda assembly line.

SUPERCHARGED CAFÉ RACER

Most riders look at the Gold Wing and see a touring bike. Phillip Sanford saw something else: potential. He started out with an '84 GL1200, and proceeded to recast it in a new mold.

Interstate luxury would be replaced with backroad agility; this Gold Wing would be a café racer, through and through. A belt-driven supercharger fed by a two-barrel carburetor supplies additional thrust. Sport-tuned suspension components, a low handlebar and probably the only set of rear-set foot controls you'll ever see on a Gold Wing complete the functional modifications on Sanford's bike.

The cosmetic enhancements are at least as impressive. From the front of the small fairing to the back of the trailer, this Wing is awash in brilliant yellow, with shocking red accents. Sanford's matching custom leathers and a custom seat complete the high-impact visual presentation. The visual excitement lasts all

night long, as seven purple neon lights bathe the Wing in an eerie glow.

Based in Nolensville, Tennessee, Sanford rides to rallies throughout the country, where he sheds his luggage-filled trailer and heads out in search of meandering backroads. He admits remorselessly to "getting kinda carried away" with his Café Gold Wing project. And there's no letup in sight. Sanford has 13 more motorcycles awaiting restoration or modification out in his shed.

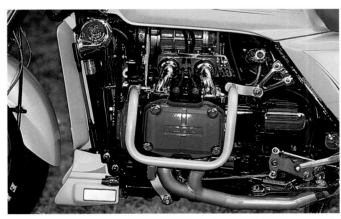

"YOU LET A TOURING BIKE PASS YOU?" "YEAH, but this wasn't any ordinary Gold Wing!" Supercharging is only one of the many extremes to which Phillip Sanford took his 1984 GL1200.

GERMAN GL

Is this a custom George Barris version of the Gold Wing? Not quite. This is the German GL built in Marysville, Ohio. The most visible distinction from its U.S. counterpart is the bike's shorter windscreen and abbreviated rear trunk, which give the bike a far more aggressive profile.

ARTIST'S CONCEPT SHOWS JUST HOW RUSS Collins envisioned taking flight on his 600-horsepower, 2000cc, supercharged, fuel-injected inline-four with GL1100 heads.

BATTLESTAR

Russ Collins ruled the quarter-mile in the 1970s. His series of two- and three-engine Top-Fuel Honda drag bikes set ever-escalating records for terminal speed in the 440-yard standing-start dash. Coming within a whisker of touching the magical 200-mph mark in less than seven seconds, these machines put on a tremendous show.

Led by increasing safety concerns, Top-Fuelers were limited to just one engine in the early '80s, prompting Collins to envision an all-new motorcycle that would borrow key concepts from Top-Fuel drag racing cars. Instead of placing the rider above the engine motorcycle-style, the wheelbase would be extended out to more than 11 feet, and the rider would be stretched out in front of the engine, low to the ground. The superior weight distribution would milk the most traction out of the enormous 15-inch-wide racing slick.

The rules allowed the motorcycle to be built from scratch, with the exception of the cylinder heads, which had to be production-based motorcycle components. Collins reached for the most appropriate heads in the Honda inventory at the time—those of the GL1100 Gold Wing. Bolted to the top of a scratch-built, 2000cc, supercharged, fuel-injected, inline-four, the combination was good for about 600 horsepower.

Collins' theories on chassis design were validated in early practices, when the Battlestar proved to be a docile handler by Top-Fuel standards. But the power to run at and above the required 200 mph simply wasn't there. The Battlestar's best runs were in the low 180-mph range, with elapsed times of 7.8 seconds—about a half-second slower than the class best of the time. With no hope of extracting further horsepower from the engine, the world's quickest Gold Wing was retired before it ever saw competition.

BIG RIG TRAILER

Gold Wingers have done much to elevate the lowly trailer from mere servant to a new-age art form. GWRRA members, Clifford and Patricia Collins, created this miniature Kenworth dump truck—complete with running lights and CB antenna—to haul behind their GL1500. Passing truckers have been known to refer to it as "that little bitty dump truck."

ALL THE COMFORTS OF HOME

Though getting away from it all is a prime motivation for many tourers, some simply can't resist bringing all the comforts of home along with them. Malcolm Cummings' awesome GL1500-based sculpture, named "Lil' Yeller," is outfitted with nearly every imaginable modern convenience. Besides some of the most outrageous bodywork ever to grace a Gold Wing, the bike is slated to be fitted with many of the amenities found on his previous creation, "Ole Yeller." These include an on-board VCR and camcorder, CB radio, and a six-speaker stereo system. The burglar alarm talks—and so does the kickstand. Really.

NO, IT'S NOT A DISNEYLAND RIDE, ALTHOUGH WALT might wish he'd thought of it first. There's no kitchen sink yet, but give Malcolm Cummings a little more time.

THE FLYING WING

The tremendous reliability of the Gold Wing engine makes it appealing to more than just motorcyclists. Aerospace machinist Leonard Haman of H&H Engineering, in Portales, New Mexico, thought that maybe home-built aircraft could benefit from a dose of Gold Wing durability, and he set out to modify the 1000 and 1100cc engines for aircraft use.

"Everybody is sold on the reliability of the Gold Wing," Haman says. His 86-horsepower conversion of the engine is aimed at a very active segment of the home-built, kit-plane market. Haman overhauls used engines (though he says they invariably look new inside), removes the transmission, then fits his own CNC-machined propeller drive assembly, which employs many of the stock transmission parts. "The qualities of the materials in this engine are the best I've seen," he reports.

Haman's creation will be fitted to a Seabird amphibian for its first flight, a prospect he faces without a whit of trepidation. On the road, Haman is a V-twin man. But as he puts it, " When it comes to my flying, I've got to get real."

THROUGH THE EFFORTS OF LEONARD HAMAN, Honda's GL1000 and 1100 engines finally get real wings with which to fly.

*F*or every rider, there's a point when a tour officially starts. For

some, it begins with the sorting and packing a motorcycle tour

requires, or scouring a map for the route. For others, it starts when

they click the transmission into high gear just past the final stop-

light in town. Still others don't feel they've made the break until

the last hometown radio station fades to a garbled mix of static

and unintelligible phrases.

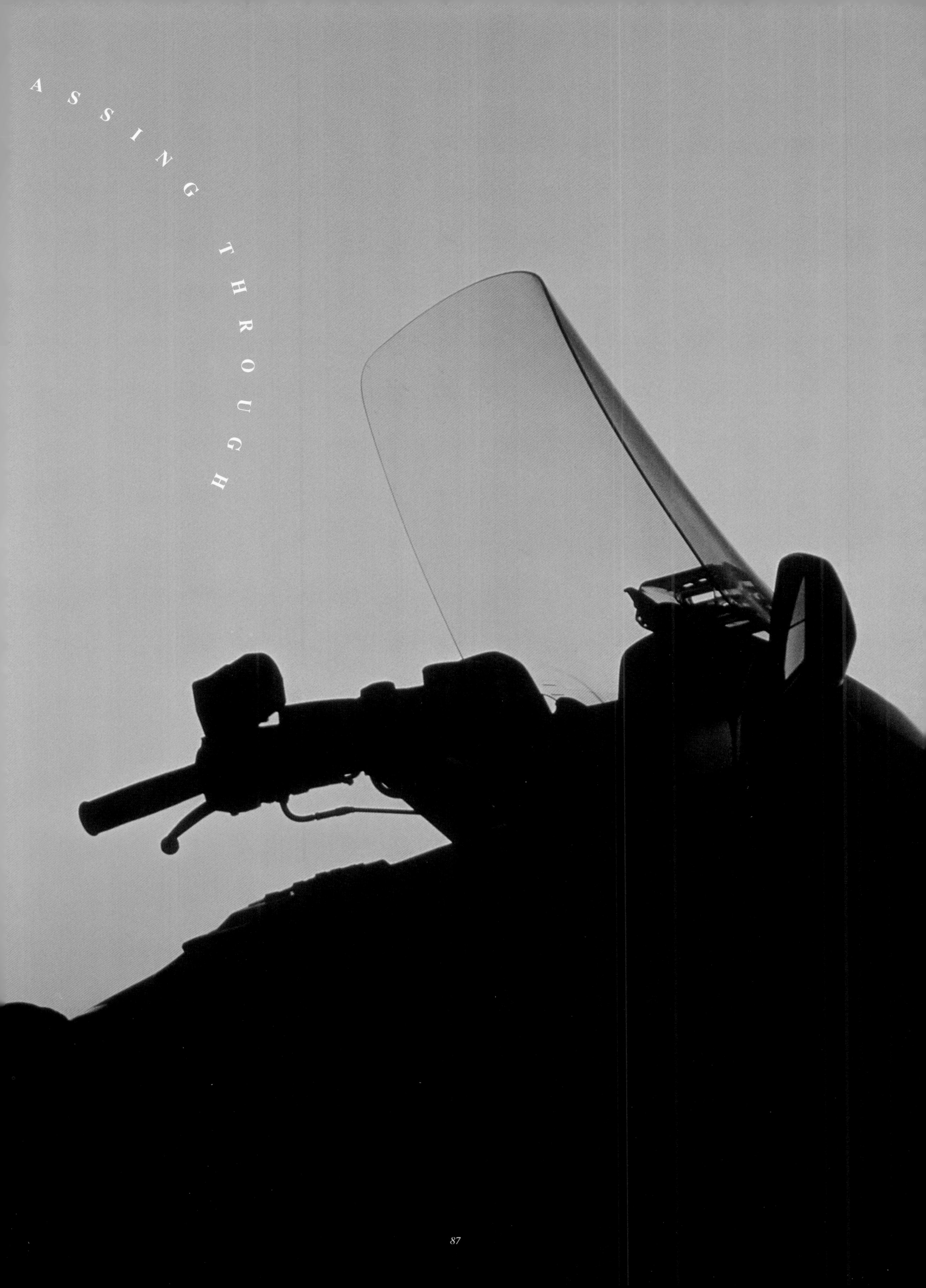
ASSING THROUGH

For some riders, the official start of a tour is not so well defined. Rather than a preset occurrence, it's more a simple realization: the first chill seeping into pant cuffs or up shirt sleeves as the sun sets. Or the wet scent of early morning mist shrouding some wandering bit of two-lane.

It's these last two that cut straight to the heart of motorcycle touring. This isn't merely travel. On a bike, you don't pass through the countryside, you're involved with it. Unlike a traveler cosseted in the climate-controlled cabin of a car, who views his passage like some extended IMax video, a motorcycle rider isn't a detached observer. Motorcycles engage all your senses. Whether it's

**TOURING RIDERS IN GENERAL,
and Gold Wing riders in particular,
tend to be colorful characters who
delight in showing off their event pins,
and they revel in the memory of miles.**

dropping into the welcome cool of a shaded valley or a whiff of cigarette smoke from a passing car, a motorcycle immerses you in the scenery. You're no longer a passive voyeur, you're an active participant.

Maybe that's why motorcycle touring memories snap into focus with an accuracy that makes photos in an album seem fuzzy. The page opens to a Maine panorama, with a solitary fisherman surrounded by a broad, clear plane of blue water, his fly rod raised and flyline etching a lazy S into the morning sky. But the picture is only part of the memory; the scent of damp leaves and the warmth of the New England sun on your shoulders rush back with equal immediacy.

Another page finds you in the cold fall of the New Mexico mountains, the sheer red-rock faces of surrounding buttes drawn in stark relief by your Wing's headlight. The strength of the night's piercing chill is broken by a single glance upward, where the stars litter the sky like grains of salt on a black tablecloth, burning brightly enough to illuminate the road.

Years later, it's the view that sparks the remembrance; the cold comes only in afterthought, but still freezes the memory in place.

Psychologists note that auditory and olfactory memories are the strongest, so in a sense, sounds and smells become our tickets to time travel. The heady aroma of salty air on the rim of the Pacific, or the smell of

an Ozark mountain smokehouse, or even the crunch of gravel in a Yosemite parking lot draws us back to the moment. This is what makes touring memories so strong—and so precious. You don't merely remember it: You're *there*.

Because they welcome the elements, motorcycles serve up this sensory smorgasbord with generous portions. Every great road has a rhythm all its own, but it's a rare car that can bring it out. Your Gold Wing does it as a matter of course. As the bike banks to follow the sweep of a winding roadway, it describes your course like no road map can.

As you become more aware, these perceptions sift down to minute detail. Gloved fingers can't dull the bite of the tires as you arc through a corner. The tinkle of loose gravel warns you about a recently repaved road, while the smell of fresh tar confirms the warning. Stripped of a car's hermetic cocoon, we become free to experience the country alfresco.

Because we become so directly connected with our surroundings, their effect on us becomes even more profound. A slow ride through a Vicksburg battlefield evokes a torrent of feelings, as a respect for history mutes our voice and suppresses our hand at the throttle. We pass through, and the connection between our past and present becomes somehow more direct.

It's no surprise the open road becomes so seductive. A ride through the flat lands of western Kansas tempts us to stay in the saddle, with the approaching Rocky Mountains measuring our progress. The sweeping California coast near San Simeon makes us hold out for the rugged beauty of Big Sur farther north. Comfortably seated behind the protection of the Wing's fairing, we hold out for the next mile, the next new experience.

And while we may wax poetic about the perfect days, we can also revel in the bad ones. There's something about touring that makes us suffer the elements—rain, cold, even snow—and feel better about ourselves in overcoming them. This is something unknown to other travelers, who spend their

time insulated from such exposure, and isolated from our experience. Away from the protection of environment controls, we take immense comfort in the simple pleasures of a warm jacket, dry boots, a clear face shield and a good fairing. Surrounded by these simple luxuries, we motor on.

Overcoming the elements involves us more closely with our trip, even before it starts. Long-distance motorcycle touring requires more than a full suitcase, a tank of gas and a wallet full of credit cards. Weather conditions and seasons dictate destinations and routes, and planning becomes an integral part of a tour. From the outset, motor-

cycles demand our complete involvement, requiring us to consider

everything from routes to rain gear.

Touring makes us collectors, for a trip by motorcycle gathers intangibles: visions and sensations we keep for ourselves, recollections we save to pass on to others. A twisting highway clinging to the emerald green Oregon coast becomes our private postcard. File it away. A biting Vermont cold may make us wish for home—even though it's a thousand miles away—yet the chance to reminisce makes us smile at the memory. Keep this as well.

The same elements that make us savor our own experience draw us together with others who share the road. For those who travel with us, the days are filled with opportunities to secure the bond. For motorcyclists who pass us by, a simple upraised hand provides the link. After several days on the road, the warm, familiar glow of the Wing's cockpit takes on a stronger significance; *this* is home, and these are our neighbors.

For a companion who shares your saddle, the intimacy of a Gold Wing draws you even closer. Unlike a car, which separates its occupants with consoles and bucket seats, a motorcycle places its riders in constant contact.

This closeness is continuously reaffirmed, as the touch of a hand or the

brush of a thigh underscores the bond between rider and passenger.

But the strongest connection exists between the rider and the road.

Maybe that's why the lure of the open road seems to tug a little harder for

those who have traveled it by motorcycle. For only they know there is no

better view of the country than over a pair of handgrips. And no matter

how we view the beginning of our tours, they all end the same way—

with plans for the next one.

Landmark Models

HOW HONDA HAS SEEN—AND SHOWN—THE MOST IMPORTANT
GOLD WINGS, IN PRINT ADS AND BROCHURES.

1975 GL1000 brochure

The first brochure for the first-year GL1000 shows how important Honda thought the bike was—and how proud the company was of it. The cover plainly sets the stage, listing the five most important models of the previous 27 years, so that you'd know the GL was in some pretty special company. And the inside, with the full-profile shot of the bike and a dozen effusive quotes from magazines worldwide, reinforces how revolutionary the Gold Wing was.

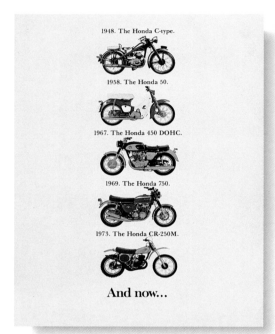

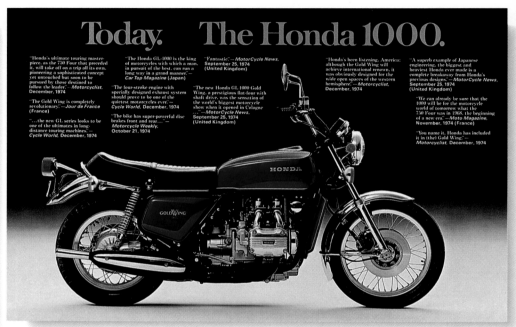

1980 GL1100 Interstate ad

The way we—and Honda—were. With this ad, Honda uses extensive copy to extol the virtues of the first Interstate, the Gold Wing that ushered in the era of turn-key touring. "The Interstate of the Art," the headline says, followed by "The Gold Wing Interstate. A motorcycle justifiably named for the road it owns." And the tag line? "Because the Interstate is more than merely a machine. It is art." And there we are as Honda envisioned us: young, in love, and ready for the jump to hyperspace in hip silver Hondaline touring suits.

1982 GL1100 Aspencade ad

If the Interstate brought us turn-key touring, the Aspencade in 1982 swept us into the realm of luxury touring. Here, call-outs draw our attention to the Aspencade's many features. "It not only comes with everything you can imagine," the copy says, "it comes with things you can't possibly imagine. Because we just invented them."

1982 GL1100 Aspencade Redpages

Honda has always been a technological leader, and to reinforce that notion the firm ran a series of ads called Redpages in the '70s and '80s; these two for the Aspencade's digital instruments and on-board air compressor are perfect examples. Redpages did more than merely tout features. They explained the innovative technology, and in so doing helped educate motorcyclists.

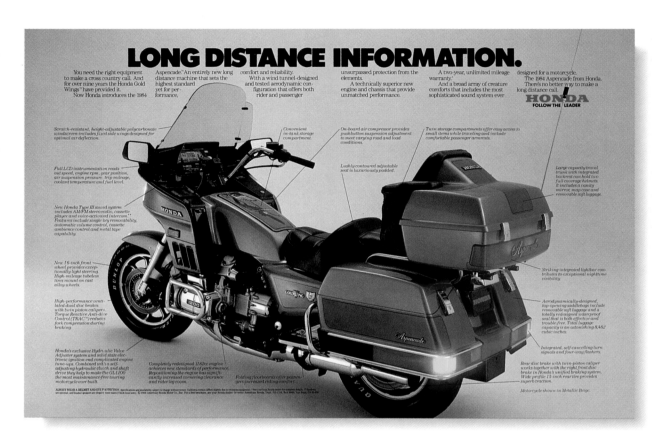

1984 GL1200 Aspencade ad

Reminiscent of the ads for the Interstate and the Aspencade, this one for the then-new GL1200 combines the elements of both. There's the catchy head—"Long Distance Information"—and numerous call-outs for the bike's myriad features.

1985 GL1200 Limited Edition ad

The Gold Wing has always been one of Honda's maximum expressions, and few more so than the 1985 Limited Edition model. Unlike most Gold Wing ads, this one shows two overall views of the bike, with five details of the long list of standard equipment on the Limited.

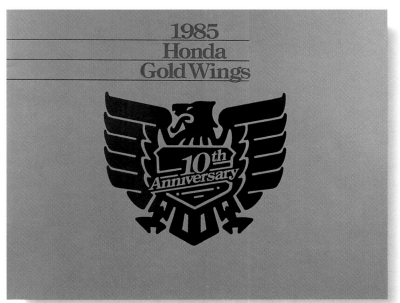

1985 brochure

For the Gold Wing's 10th anniversary, Honda produced an elaborately printed brochure, with lengthy, detailed copy on each model. Naturally, the most lavish display went to the Limited Edition, the most remarkable expression of luxury touring of the day.

Introducing
The Gold Wing
Limited Edition.

1988 GL1500 ad

In 1988, Honda unveiled the incredible, luxurious, six-cylinder GL1500 Gold Wing. The advertising that accompanied the bike was elegant and understated, with copy highlighting its features, and photography that focused on the bike's ergonomic accommodations.

Designing motorcycles is like touring. The further you go, the better it gets.

There's nothing quite like touring on two wheels. Traveling through a winding canyon. Powering over a mountain pass. Breathing the salt air as you cruise the coastline. Exploring America. The Honda Gold Wing® was created for just such moments.

The Gold Wing's clean, sculptured look can be attributed in part to extensive wind tunnel testing. To minimize even the slightest amount of drag, all exterior latches were removed and a unique integrated locking system was created. The luggage compartments were also redesigned to maximize storage space, resulting in the most usable storage room of any touring motorcycle.

To maximize rider and passenger comfort, the Gold Wing's seat has been completely redesigned to strike a perfect balance between support and comfort. Honda engineers tested dozens of seats before coming up with the ultimate design. And then they turned their attention to still more improvements.

For 1988, several significant advances were made in the area of air management. The Gold Wing's fairing and windshield have been aerodynamically designed to create an envelope of still air around the rider and passenger at cruising speeds. In addition, the windshield can be easily lowered or raised to accommodate the rider's height. To keep both rider and passenger comfortable in any kind of weather, vents can be adjusted to route cool or warm air as needed. And to ensure that you only get warm air when you want it, the Gold Wing's engine is enclosed by bodywork which keeps engine and exhaust heat away from the rider.

The Gold Wing is powered by a revolutionary new 1520cc flat-six engine. It's smoother, quieter and provides more torque than any other touring motorcycle.

The 1988 Gold Wing is taking touring in a new direction. Backwards. In response to rider requests, Honda engineers outfitted the Gold Wing with a motorized electric reverse. In doing so, they've brought a new level of maneuverability to the touring class. Of course, reverse is only one example of this year's advances.

For your listening pleasure, the Gold Wing features a 24-watt am/fm stereo cassette system with integrated intercom. All controls are designed to be adjustable by a gloved hand and are easily within the rider's reach.

The 1988 Honda Gold Wing is built in America for worldwide distribution. In terms of performance, comfort and value, it represents the furthest a touring motorcycle has ever been taken. To experience it firsthand, visit your nearest Honda dealer.

WINNERS RIDE SAFELY. Don't take chances. Professional motorcyclists ride to win. And they know they can't win if they don't finish. The pros also know how responsible riding practices and the proper safety equipment help them finish by minimizing risks. They ride accordingly, and so should you.

Use the proper equipment. Pros always use quality helmets, eye protection and protective clothing, just as all motorcyclists and their passengers should. And the pros realize no one should ever operate any motor vehicle while under the influence of alcohol or drugs. **Make every ride an education.** Pros too good. The Motorcycle Safety Foundation knows know every safe rider is a winner, and that no rider is ever For more information, call them at 1-800-447-4700. that too, and they offer classes to help you improve your skills or see your local Honda dealer.

HONDA
Come ride with us.

Specifications and availability subject to change without notice. †See your local Honda dealer for complete details. California version differs slightly due to emissions equipment. For a free brochure, see your Honda dealer. Or write: American Honda, Dept. 528, P.O. Box 7013, No. Hollywood, CA 91609-7013. Gold Wing is a registered Honda trademark. ©1988 American Honda Motor Co., Inc. (5/88)

CHARTING THE CHANGES IN THE GOLD WING'S 20-YEAR

OLD WING SPOTTER'S GUIDE

EVOLUTION TAKES A CAREFUL EYE. WHILE A FEW

CHANGES HAVE BEEN SUDDEN AND OBVIOUS, MOST ARE

HARDER TO SPOT. THE FOLLOWING GUIDE MAKES IT EASIER

TO TELL ONE YEAR AND MODEL FROM ANOTHER USING

KEY SPECIFICATIONS AND FEATURES.

DARWIN NEVER

HAD IT SO

EASY.

The original GL1000 Gold Wing, powered by a 999cc liquid-cooled, horizontally opposed four-cylinder engine, revolutionized motorcycle touring. The *faux* fuel tank contains electrical components and storage space. Spoked aluminum rims are standard. Note the black exhaust system, with chrome heat shields and tailpipes.

1975 GL1000

1975 GL1000

Suggested retail	$2881 (East), $2899 (West)
Engine type	OHC opposed-four, liquid-cooled
Displacement	999cc
Carburetion	(4) 32mm CV
Starting system	Electric plus kick
Transmission	Five-speed
Final drive	Shaft
Chassis	Steel, dual shock
Front brake	Dual-disc, single-piston caliper
Rear brake	Single-disc, single-piston caliper
Wheelbase	60.6 in.
Seat height	31.9 in.
Fuel capacity	5.0 gal.
Dry weight	584.0 lb.
Color	Candy Red, Candy Blue

A new **1976 GL1000** model marks the Gold Wing's second year. **1976 GL1000 LTD** The GL1000 LTD joins the unchanged standard model, and features gold striping, special LTD sidecover badges, chromed radiator shroud and screen, quilt-pattern contoured seat, gold wheels and spokes, gold-stamped GL1000 owner's manual, and leather key case. The LTD's front fender is slightly flared.

1976 GL1000 •
GL1000 LTD ↔
Suggested retail ....$2960 (East), $2942 (West) •
.................................$3295 ↔
Engine type ....OHC opposed-four, liquid-cooled
Displacement 999cc
Carburetion ....(4) 32mm CV
Starting system ....Electric plus kick
Transmission ....Five-speed
Final drive ....Shaft
Chassis ....Steel, dual shock
Front brake ....Dual-disc, single-piston caliper
Rear brake ....Single-disc, single-piston caliper
Wheelbase ....60.8 in.
Seat height ....31.9 in.
Fuel capacity ....5.0 gal.
Dry weight ....583.0 lb.
Color ....Candy Red, Solid Yellow •
.................................Candy Brown ↔

Honda **1977 GL1000** begins to incorporate small but important refinements based on customer requests, as the Gold Wing continues to grow in popularity and redefine touring. Chrome heat shields on the header pipes are now standard, as is a higher, recontoured handlebar, redesigned neoprene grips, and a new dual contoured seat.

1977 GL1000
Suggested retail $2938
Engine type ....OHC opposed-four, liquid-cooled
Displacement 999cc
Carburetion ....(4) 32mm CV
Starting system ....Electric plus kick
Transmission ....Five-speed
Final drive ....Shaft
Chassis ....Steel, dual shock
Front brake ....Dual-disc, single-piston caliper
Rear brake ....Single-disc, single-piston caliper
Wheelbase ....60.8 in.
Seat height ....31.9 in.
Fuel capacity ....5.0 gal.
Dry weight ....595.0 lb.
Color ....Black, Red

A new instru- **1978 GL1000** ment panel in the center pod with fuel, voltage and coolant temperature gauges helps distinguish the GL in its fourth year. Honda also fitted 1mm-smaller carbs and FVQ™ shocks with two-stage damping, redesigned and chromed the exhaust system, mounted the rear turn signals on the fender, deleted the kick-starter, and bolted up maintenance-free ComStar wheels.

1978 GL1000
Suggested retail $3198
Engine type ....OHC opposed-four, liquid-cooled
Displacement 999cc
Carburetion ....(4) 31mm CV
Starting system ....Electric
Transmission ....Five-speed
Final drive ....Shaft
Chassis ....Steel, dual shock
Front brake ....Dual-disc, single-piston caliper
Rear brake ....Single-disc, single-piston caliper
Wheelbase ....60.8 in.
Seat height ....31.9 in.
Fuel capacity ....5.0 gal.
Dry weight ....601.0 lb.
Color ....Blue, Maroon, Black

The GL1000 **1979 GL1000** reaches the peak of its development in 1979, and will be the last Gold Wing to be powered by a 999cc engine. Changes this year are few and minor: Rectangular turn signals replace the previous round ones, control levers go from silver to black, and a twin-bulb taillight with CBX-type ribbed lens replaces the single-bulb unit.

1979 GL1000
Suggested retail $3698
Engine type ....OHC opposed-four, liquid-cooled
Displacement 999cc
Carburetion ....(4) 31mm CV
Starting system ....Electric
Transmission ....Five-speed
Final drive ....Shaft
Chassis ....Steel, dual shock
Front brake ....Dual-disc, single-piston caliper
Rear brake ....Single-disc, single-piston caliper
Wheelbase ....60.8 in.
Seat height ....31.9 in.
Fuel capacity ....5.0 gal.
Dry weight ....604.0 lb.
Color ....Candy Burgundy,
.................................Candy Blue, Black

The introduction of the second-generation GL sees the  standard version joined by the first Japanese turn-key tourer, the Interstate model. Both are powered by a new 1085cc engine with electronic ignition—no more points. The chassis boasts air suspension with a single-inlet equalizer system at each end, black reverse ComStar wheels, adjustable seat, and bigger tires. The Interstate sets new standards for touring with its full fairing, saddlebags and trunk, and optional stereo.

1980 GL1100
1980 GL1100 INTERSTATE

1980 GL1100 •
GL1100 INTERSTATE ••
Suggested retail ....$3798 •, $4898 ••
Engine type ....OHC opposed-four, liquid-cooled
Displacement 1085cc
Carburetion ....(4) 30mm CV
Starting system ....Electric
Transmission ....Five-speed
Final drive ....Shaft
Chassis ....Steel, dual shock
Front brake ....Dual-disc, single-piston caliper
Rear brake ....Single-disc, single-piston caliper
Wheelbase ....63.2 in.
Seat height ....31.3 in.
Fuel capacity ....5.3 gal.
Dry weight ....586.0 lb. •, 672.5 lb. ••
Color ....Candy Burgundy, Black

Distinguished  by new orange and gold pinstripes, the standard and Interstate model GL1100s boast redesigned instruments with improved nighttime illumination. The Interstate also features a new adjustable, scratch-resistant windshield, and continues to set the pace for turn-key touring motorcycles.

1981 GL1100
1981 GL1100 INTERSTATE

1981 GL1100 •
GL1100 INTERSTATE ••
Suggested retail ....$4098 •, $5298 ••
Engine type ....OHC opposed-four, liquid-cooled
Displacement 1085cc
Carburetion ....(4) 30mm CV
Starting system ....Electric
Transmission ....Five-speed
Final drive ....Shaft
Chassis ....Steel, dual shock
Front brake ....Dual-disc, single-piston caliper
Rear brake ....Single-disc, single-piston caliper
Wheelbase ....63.2 in.
Seat height ....31.3 in.
Fuel capacity ....5.3 gal.
Dry weight ....588.7 lb. •, 672.5 lb. ••
Color ....Candy Burgundy, Metallic Blue Black

For '82, Honda  adds a third model to the GL line, the even more luxurious Aspencade. The Interstate model offers such options as a new Type II stereo, a 40-channel CB transceiver, and an on-board air compressor. All of these items are standard on the Aspencade, as are storage pouches in the passenger backrest, two-tone paint and seat, and special-edition Aspencade badges. All models also sport twin-piston brake calipers and wider tires.

1982 GL1100
1982 GL1100 INTERSTATE
1982 GL1100 ASPENCADE

1982 GL1100 •
GL1100 INTERSTATE ••
GL1100 ASPENCADE •••
Suggested retail ....$4248 •, $5448 ••, $5698 •••
Engine type ....OHC opposed-four, liquid-cooled
Displacement 1085cc
Carburetion ....(4) 30mm CV
Starting system ....Electric
Transmission ....Five-speed
Final drive ....Shaft
Chassis ....Steel, dual shock
Front brake ....Dual-disc, twin-piston caliper
Rear brake ....Single-disc, twin-piston caliper
Wheelbase ....63.2 in.
Seat height ....31.1 in.
Fuel capacity ....5.3 gal.
Dry weight ....595.4 lb. •, 679.1 lb. ••, 702.3 lb •••
Color ....Wineberry Red, Black, Metallic Black • ••
Metallic Brown, Metallic Silver •••

The last year  for the GL1100s finds them fitted with 11-spoke cast wheels, TRAC anti-dive fork with an integrated fork brace, and unified braking system. The Interstate adds larger, flatter footpegs and adjustable passenger pegs, while the top-of-the-line Aspencade also boasts internally vented front brake rotors, a digital LCD instrument panel and a new two-tone seat.

1983 GL1100
1983 INTERSTATE
1983 ASPENCADE

1983 GL1100 •
GL1100 INTERSTATE ••
GL1100 ASPENCADE •••
Suggested retail ....$4298 •, $5548 ••, $6998 •••
Engine type ....OHC opposed-four, liquid-cooled
Displacement 1085cc
Carburetion ....(4) 30mm CV
Starting system ....Electric
Transmission ....Five-speed
Final drive ....Shaft
Chassis ....Steel, dual shock
Front brake ....Dual-disc, twin-piston caliper
Rear brake ....Single-disc, twin-piston caliper
Wheelbase ....63.2 in.
Seat height ....31.1 in.
Fuel capacity ....5.3 gal.
Dry weight ....599.8 lb. •, 685.8 lb. ••, 707.8 lb. •••
Color ....Black, Candy Regal Brown • ••
Candy Wineberry Red, Metallic Gray •••

This year sees the Wing once again rewrite the rules for touring, with the all-new GL1200s. All three models are motivated by a new, 1182cc engine with hydraulic valve adjustment, and a redesigned chassis sports a 16-inch front wheel for steering lightness and precision previously unseen in the class. The Aspencade distinguishes itself from the Interstate with LCD instruments and special rear lightbar, as well as a new Type III audio system that combines AM/FM radio bands, cassette and intercom.

1984 GL1200 •
GL1200 INTERSTATE ••
GL1200 ASPENCADE •••
Suggested retail ....$4795 •, $6195 ••, $7895 •••
Engine type ....OHC opposed-four, liquid-cooled
Displacement 1182cc
Carburetion ....(4) 32mm CV
Starting system ......Electric
Transmission ....Five-speed
Final drive ....Shaft
Chassis ....Steel, dual shock
Front brake ....Dual-disc, twin-piston caliper
Rear brake ....Single-disc, twin-piston caliper
Wheelbase ....63.4 in.
Seat height ....30.7 in.
Fuel capacity ....5.8 gal.
Dry weight ....599.8 lb. •, 701.2 lb. ••, 723.3 lb. •••
Color ....Wineberry Red, Black •
                          Wineberry Red,
                          Metallic Gray, Pearl Blue ••
                          Burgundy, Pearl Blue,
                          Metallic Beige •••

With the surge in touring's popularity, Honda drops the standard Gold Wing in '85, but a top-of-the-line LTD model joins the Aspencade and Interstate, once again raising the ante for touring opulence. The GL1200L Limited Edition comes with computerized fuel injection, Type III audio/intercom system with four speakers, cruise control, auto-leveling rear suspension and a comprehensive electronic travel computer.

1985 GL1200 INTERSTATE •
GL1200 ASPENCADE ••
GL1200 LIMITED EDITION •••
Suggested retail ....$6198 •, $7898 ••, $10,000 •••
Engine type ....OHC opposed-four, liquid-cooled
Displacement 1182cc
Carburetion ....(4) 32mm CV • ••,
                          Computerized fuel injection •••
Starting system ....Electric
Transmission ....Five-speed
Final drive ....Shaft
Chassis ....Steel, dual shock
Front brake ....Dual-disc, twin-piston caliper
Rear brake ....Single-disc, twin-piston caliper
Wheelbase ....63.4 in.
Seat height ....30.7 in.
Fuel capacity ....5.8 gal.
Dry weight ....699.0 lb. •, 727.7 lb. ••, 771.8 lb. •••
Color ....Metallic Silver, Metallic Blue,
                          Wineberry Red •
                          Metallic Beige, Metallic Blue,
                          Vintage Red ••, Metallic Gold •••

Few changes distinguish the GL1200s for their third year of production. The Limited Edition gets renamed the GL1200SE-i, and now features Dolby noise reduction for its Panasonic Type III sound system. The Aspencade gets the same audio update, and both Interstate and Aspencade models can be easily identified by their new rear fender splash guards.

1986 GL1200 INTERSTATE •
GL1200 ASPENCADE ••
GL1200 ASPENCADE SE-i •••
Suggested retail ....$6698 •, $8498 ••, $10,598 •••
Engine type ....OHC opposed-four, liquid-cooled
Displacement 1182cc
Carburetion ....(4) 32mm CV • ••,
                          Computerized fuel injection •••
Starting system ....Electric
Transmission ....Five-speed
Final drive ....Shaft
Chassis ....Steel, dual shock
Front brake ....Dual-disc, twin-piston caliper
Rear brake ....Single-disc, twin-piston caliper
Wheelbase ....63.4 in.
Seat height ....30.7 in.
Fuel capacity ....5.8 gal.
Dry weight ....699.0 lb. •, 727.7 lb. ••, 771.8 lb. •••
Color ....Wineberry Red, Black •
                          Metallic Beige, Metallic Blue,
                          Metallic Silver ••
                          Pearl White •••

The Gold Wing lineup gets pared to two models, the Interstate and the Aspencade, with the SE-i consigned to history. Both remaining models feature a new tapered seat design with three-stage foam, and the two differ mainly in weight and standard equipment. The Type III sound system, passenger floorboards and armrests, and a trunk mirror are standard on the Aspencade, options on the Interstate.

1987 GL1200 INTERSTATE •
GL1200 ASPENCADE ••
Suggested retail ....$6698 •, $8498 ••
Engine type ....OHC opposed-four, liquid-cooled
Displacement 1182cc
Carburetion ....(4) 32mm CV
Starting system ....Electric
Transmission ....Five-speed
Final drive ....Shaft
Chassis ....Steel, dual shock
Front brake ....Dual-disc, twin-piston caliper
Rear brake ....Single-disc, twin-piston caliper
Wheelbase ....63.4 in.
Seat height ....30.7 in.
Fuel capacity ....5.8 gal.
Dry weight ....699.0 lb. •, 743.1 lb. ••
Color ....Metallic Beige,
                          Amethyst Silver • ••
                          Wineberry Red, Black,
                          Metallic Silver ••

Honda ups  **1988 GL1500**
the ante again with the ultimate
touring bike, the fourth-genera-
tion Gold Wing GL1500 six-
cylinder. The 1520cc six sets
fresh standards of smoothness,
silence and power for the class,
while an all-new chassis rede-
fines the limits of handling and
comfort. A unique-to-motor-
cycling reverse gear and single-
key operation of the saddlebag
and trunk lids offer unparalleled
convenience.

1988 GL1500
Suggested retail	$9998
Engine type	OHC opposed-six, liquid-cooled
Displacement	1520cc
Carburetion	(2) 36mm CV
Starting system	Electric
Transmission	Five-speed
Final drive	Shaft
Chassis	Steel, dual shock
Front brake	Dual-disc, twin-piston caliper
Rear brake	Single-disc, twin-piston caliper
Wheelbase	66.9 in.
Seat height	30.3 in.
Fuel capacity	6.3 gal.
Dry weight	793.8 lb.
Color	Phantom Gray, Martini Beige, Dynastic Blue

Few alter-  **1989 GL1500**
ations are needed for such a land-
mark model, even in its second
year of production. The six
remains as a single model with
no variants. As in '88, options
include a CB radio, saddlebag
light kit, cornering light kit,
color-matched saddlebag and
trunk spoilers, color-matched
lower-leg air vents, a rear speaker
kit, a trunk light/mirror, and passenger audio controls. The 1500/6
badge is removed from the rear of
the right-side bag.

1989 GL1500
Suggested retail	$11,498
Engine type	OHC opposed-six, liquid-cooled
Displacement	1520cc
Carburetion	(2) 36mm CV
Starting system	Electric
Transmission	Five-speed
Final drive	Shaft
Chassis	Steel, dual shock
Front brake	Dual-disc, twin-piston caliper
Rear brake	Single-disc, twin-piston caliper
Wheelbase	66.9 in.
Seat height	30.3 in.
Fuel capacity	6.3 gal.
Dry weight	793.8 lb.
Color	Martini Beige, Wineberry Red, Blue Green Metallic

A new SE  **1990 GL1500**
model joins the standard
GL1500, **1990 GL1500 SE**
and both benefit from a host of
updates for 1990, including carb
and cam revisions for better
drivability, noise reductions,
even tighter bodywork fit and
finish, and smoother fork action.
The SE sports special two-tone
paint, a three-position center
windscreen vent, a special rear
trunk spoiler with running/brake
light, adjustable passenger foot-
rests, and an upgraded, full-
logic sound system.

1990 GL1500 •
GL1500 SE ••
Suggested retail	$11,498 •, $13,498 ••
Engine type	OHC opposed-six, liquid-cooled
Displacement	1520cc
Carburetion	(2) 36mm CV
Starting system	Electric
Transmission	Five-speed
Final drive	Shaft
Chassis	Steel, dual shock
Front brake	Dual-disc, twin-piston caliper
Rear brake	Single-disc, twin-piston caliper
Wheelbase	66.9 in.
Seat height	30.3 in.
Fuel capacity	6.3 gal.
Dry weight	798.0 lb. •, 804.0 lb. ••
Color	Wineberry Red, Light Metallic Blue •, Pearl White ••

Once again,  **1991 GL1500 INTERSTATE**
the Gold Wing counts three
members in **1991 GL1500 ASPENCADE**
its extended family, with the SE
joined by **1991 GL1500 SE**
Aspencade and Interstate models. The SE remains largely
unchanged for '91 save for new
two-tone gold paint, and the
Aspencade takes on the role of
the previous standard-model
GL1500. The new model, the
Interstate, features a redesigned
seat for an 0.8-inch-lower saddle
height, and 40 pounds less
weight for a sportier feel.

1991 GL1500 INTERSTATE •
GL1500 ASPENCADE ••
GL1500 SE •••
Suggested retail	$8998 •, $11,998 ••, $13,998 •••
Engine type	OHC opposed-six, liquid-cooled
Displacement	1520cc
Carburetion	(2) 36mm CV
Starting system	Electric
Transmission	Five-speed
Final drive	Shaft
Chassis	Steel, dual shock
Front brake	Dual-disc, twin-piston caliper
Rear brake	Single-disc, twin-piston caliper
Wheelbase	66.9 in.
Seat height	29.5 in. •, 30.3 in. •• •••
Fuel capacity	6.3 gal.
Dry weight	760.7 lb. •, 800.4 lb. ••, 809.2 lb. •••
Color	Beige • Black •• Gold •••

Big news **1992 GL1500 INTERSTATE** for the Gold Wing line in 1992 centers on **1992 GL1500 ASPENCADE** the Interstate, with a revised and upgraded **1992 GL1500 SE** sound system. The Panasonic unit features a 25-watt-per-channel amplifier, standard GL speakers, large and easy-to-use knobs, an intercom, a CB radio interface, a handlebar-mounted control unit, and a special input jack connector allowing the use of a portable cassette or CD player.

1992 GL1500 INTERSTATE •
GL1500 ASPENCADE ••
GL1500 SE •••
Suggested retail ....$9199 (Blue), $9399 (Red) •
$12,099 (Blue), $12,299 (Red) ••
$14,199 •••
Engine type ....OHC opposed-six, liquid-cooled
Displacement 1520cc
Carburetion ....(2) 36mm CV
Starting system ....Electric
Transmission ....Five-speed
Final drive ....Shaft
Chassis ....Steel, dual shock
Front brake ....Dual-disc, twin-piston caliper
Rear brake ....Single-disc, twin-piston caliper
Wheelbase ....66.9 in.
Seat height ....29.5 in. •, 30.3 in. •• •••
Fuel capacity ....6.3 gal.
Dry weight ....767.3 lb. •, 800.4 lb. ••, 809.2 lb. •••
Color ....Candy Red, Metallic Blue • ••
Metallic Teal •••

Each Gold **1993 GL1500 INTERSTATE** Wing model now comes in three col- **1993 GL1500 ASPENCADE** ors, with the SE benefiting from such **1993 GL1500 SE** updates as rear-mounted speakers and 40-channel CB radio that were previously optional. On the SE and the Aspencade, the cruise control now reads crankshaft speed directly for more precise road-speed control. All 1520cc six-cylinder engines now use needle bearings in their rocker-arm pivots.

1993 GL1500 INTERSTATE •,
GL1500 ASPENCADE ••, GL1500 SE •••
Suggested retail ....$9599, $9799 (Red) • $12,399,
$12,599 (Red) ••, $14,699
(Pearl White solid), $14,999 •••
Engine type ....OHC opposed-six, liquid-cooled
Displacement 1520cc
Carburetion ....(2) 36mm CV
Starting system ....Electric
Transmission ....Five-speed
Final drive ....Shaft
Chassis ....Steel, dual shock
Front brake ....Dual-disc, twin-piston caliper
Rear brake ....Single-disc, twin-piston caliper
Wheelbase ....66.9 in.
Seat height ....29.5 in. •, 30.3 in. •• •••
Fuel capacity ....6.3 gal.
Dry weight ....767.3 lb. •, 800.4 lb. ••, 813.0 lb. •••
Color ....Candy Red, Metallic Blue, Black •
Candy Red, Metallic Blue, Black ••
Metallic Teal two-tone, Pearl Blue two-tone,
Pearl White two-tone, Pearl White solid •••

Nearly two **1994 GL1500 INTERSTATE** decades after its introduction, the Gold **1994 GL1500 ASPENCADE** Wing continues to define the touring **1994 GL1500 SE** class through the process of continuous refinement. Honda again offers three models for '94, the SE in four color choices, and the Aspencade and Interstate in three choices each. The Interstate carries on in its role as the lightest member of the Wing family, the Aspencade remains the full-featured model, and the SE crowns the very top of the Wing family tree.

1994 GL1500 INTERSTATE •,
GL1500 ASPENCADE ••, GL1500 SE •••
Suggested retail ....$9999, $10,199 (Red) •
$12,999, $13,199 (Red) ••
$15,299 Pearl-White solid, $15,599 •••
Engine type ....OHC opposed-six, liquid-cooled
Displacement 1520cc
Carburetion ....(2) 36mm CV
Starting system ....Electric
Transmission ....Five-speed
Final drive ....Shaft
Chassis ....Steel, dual shock
Front brake ....Dual-disc, twin-piston caliper
Rear brake ....Single-disc, twin-piston caliper
Wheelbase ....66.9 in.
Seat height ....29.5 in. •, 30.3 in. •• •••
Fuel capacity ....6.3 gal.
Dry weight ....767.2 lb. •, 800.3 lb. ••, 813.5 lb. •••
Color ....Candy Red, Pearl Dark Teal, Black •
Candy Red, Pearl Dark Teal, Black ••
Pearl Green two-tone, Pearl Teal two-tone
Candy Red two-tone, Pearl White solid ••

Honda cele- **1995 GL1500 INTERSTATE** brates two decades of touring excellence **1995 GL1500 ASPENCADE** with the 20th Anniversary Gold Wings. The **1995 GL1500 SE** Interstate, Aspencade and SE are all distinguished by commemorative gold trim, a distinctive new headlight signature, and other styling treatments. Beneath the surface, the Gold Wings also boast a lower seat height and sporty new suspension that offers even greater agility while maintaining the Wing's legendary ride comfort.

1995 GL1500 INTERSTATE •,
GL1500 ASPENCADE ••, GL1500 SE •••
Suggested retail ....$11,199, $11,399 (Red) •
$13,999, $14,199 (Red) ••
$16,299 (White), $16,599 (Green,
Magenta), $16,799 (Red) •••
Engine type ....OHC opposed-six, liquid-cooled
Displacement 1520cc
Carburetion ....(2) 36mm CV
Starting system ....Electric
Transmission ....Five-speed
Final drive ....Shaft
Chassis ....Steel, dual shock
Front brake ....Dual-disc, twin-piston caliper
Rear brake ....Single-disc, twin-piston caliper
Wheelbase ....66.5 in.
Seat height ....29.1 in.
Fuel capacity ....6.3 gal.
Dry weight ....769.4 lb. •, 802.5 lb. ••, 815.7 lb. •••
Color ....Candy Red, Pearl Green •
Candy Red, Pearl Green, Pearl Magenta ••
Candy Red two-tone, Pearl Green two-tone,
Pearl Magenta two-tone, Pearl White solid •••

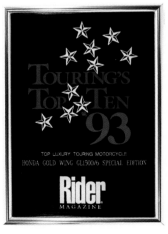

ACCOLADES

OVER THE YEARS, THE GOLD WING HAS BEEN REC-OGNIZED BY THE MOTORING MEDIA AS ONE OF THE MOST SIG-NIFICANT MOTORCYCLES OF OUR TIME, AND IT HAS THE RECORD TO PROVE IT.

CYCLE MAGAZINE

Benchmark Bikes 1991

CYCLE WORLD MAGAZINE

Best Touring Bike 1980
Best Touring Bike 1981
Best Touring Bike 1982
Best Touring Bike 1984
Best Touring Bike 1985
Best Touring Bike 1986
Best Touring Bike 1987
Best Touring Bike 1988
Best Touring Bike 1989
Best Touring Bike 1990
Best Touring Bike 1991
10 Best Motorcycles 1990
10 Greatest Bikes of All Time 1988
Readers' Choice Award—
Best Touring Bike 1991

MOTORCYCLIST MAGAZINE

Motorcycle of the Year 1988
Best Touring Bike 1989
10 Best Buys 1991
Best Full-Dress Tourer...................1990
Best Full-Dress Tourer...................1991
Best Full-Dress Tourer...................1992
Best Full-Dress Tourer...................1993
Best Full-Dress Tourer...................1994

RIDER MAGAZINE

Top Luxury Touring Motorcycle ...1990
Top Luxury Touring Motorcycle ...1991
Top Luxury Touring Motorcycle ...1992
Top Luxury Touring Motorcycle ...1993
Top Luxury Touring Motorcycle ...1994

ROAD TEST INDEX

CYCLE MAGAZINE

GL1000 Gold Wing..April 1975
GL1000 Gold Wing ....Comparison.......August 1975
GL1000 Gold Wing..March 1977
GL1000 Gold Wing..March 1978
GL1100 Gold Wing..January 1980
GL1100I Gold Wing Interstate ....September 1981
GL1100A Gold Wing Aspencade...August 1982
GL1100A Gold Wing Aspencade.......................................December 1982
GL1200A Gold Wing Aspencade..February 1984
GL1200L Gold Wing Limited Edition ....February 1985
GL1200SE-i Gold Wing Aspencade SE-i...........................January 1986
GL1500 Gold Wing..March 1988
GL1500 Gold Wing ....Comparison.......October 1988
GL1500I Gold Wing Interstate....................Comparison.......March 1991
GL1500SE Gold Wing SE...........................Comparison.......March 1991

CYCLE GUIDE MAGAZINE

GL1000 Gold Wing..April 1975
GL1000 Gold Wing..November 1977
GL1000 Gold Wing ....Comparison.......August 1979
GL1100I Gold Wing Interstate ....March 1980
GL1100I Gold Wing Interstate....................Comparison.......August 1980
GL1100I Gold Wing Interstate....................Comparison.......August 1981
GL1100 Gold Wing..April 1982
GL1100I Gold Wing Interstate ....April 1982
GL1100A Gold Wing Aspencade...April 1982
GL1100A Gold Wing Aspencade.......................................February 1983
GL1200A Gold Wing Aspencade ....Comparison.......March 1984
GL1200L Gold Wing Limited Edition ....March 1985
GL1200A Gold Wing Aspencade ....Comparison.......May 1986

CYCLE WORLD MAGAZINE

GL1000 Gold Wing..April 1975
GL1000 Gold Wing..July 1977
GL1000 Gold Wing..October 1978
GL1100 Gold Wing..April 1980
GL1100I Gold Wing Interstate....................Comparison.......May 1980
GL1100A Gold Wing Aspencade...July 1983
GL1200A Gold Wing Aspencade...March 1984
GL1200L Gold Wing Limited Edition ....Comparison.......April 1985
GL1200L Gold Wing Limited Edition ....Comparison.......August 1985
GL1200SE-i Gold Wing Aspencade SE-i ...Comparison.......June 1986
GL1500 Gold Wing..May 1988
GL1500SE Gold Wing SE...........................Comparison.......May 1990

MOTORCYCLIST MAGAZINE

GL1000 Gold Wing..May 1975
GL1100 Gold Wing..February 1980
GL1100I Gold Wing Interstate...................Comparison.......June 1980
GL1100A Gold Wing Aspencade...June 1982
GL1100I Gold Wing Interstate...................Comparison.......July 1983
GL1200A Gold Wing Aspencade...March 1984
GL1200A Gold Wing Aspencade ....Comparison.......September 1984
GL1200L Gold Wing Limited Edition ....March 1985
GL1200A Gold Wing Aspencade...October 1985
GL1200A Gold Wing Aspencade...March 1987
GL1500 Gold Wing..February 1988
GL1500I Gold Wing Interstate ....February 1991

RIDER MAGAZINE

GL1000 Gold Wing..Summer 1975
GL1000 Gold Wing..February 1977
GL1000 Gold Wing ....Comparison.......April 1978
GL1000 Gold Wing..April 1978
GL1100I Gold Wing Interstate ....July 1980
GL1100I Gold Wing Interstate...................Comparison.......August 1981
GL1100A Gold Wing Aspencade...May 1982
GL1100A Gold Wing Aspencade...June 1983
GL1200A Gold Wing Aspencade...February 1984
GL1200A Gold Wing Aspencade ....Comparison.......April 1984
GL1200L Gold Wing Limited Edition ....Comparison.......June 1985
GL1200SE-i Gold Wing Aspencade SE-i...........................January 1986
GL1200A Gold Wing Aspencade ....Comparison.......September 1987
GL1200I Gold Wing Interstate...................Comparison.......July 1987
GL1500 Gold Wing..March 1988
GL1500 Gold Wing ....Comparison.......October 1988
GL1500 Gold Wing ....Comparison.......July 1989
GL1500SE Gold Wing SE...March 1990
GL1500I Gold Wing Interstate ....January 1991
GL1500SE Gold Wing SE...........................Comparison.......April 1992
GL1500I Gold Wing Interstate ....April 1992
GL1500SE Gold Wing SE...March 1993

ROAD RIDER/MOTORCYCLE CONSUMER NEWS MAGAZINE

GL1000 Gold Wing..July 1975
GL1000 Gold Wing..July 1978
GL1100I Gold Wing Interstate ....September 1980
GL1100A Gold Wing Aspencade...June 1982
GL1200A Gold Wing Aspencade...March 1984
GL1200I Gold Wing Interstate ....March 1986
GL1500 Gold Wing..April 1988
GL1500 Gold Wing..March 1989
GL1500 Gold Wing..June 1990
GL1500I Gold Wing Interstate ....December 1991
GL1500SE Gold Wing SE...February 1993